BEST
NEWSPAPER
WRITING
1990

EDITED BY DON FRY AND KAREN BROWN

Winners: American Society of Newspaper Editors Competition

Copies of *Best Newspaper Writing 1990* are available for
$10.95 each from The Poynter Institute. Earlier editions are
also available in limited quantities. Please write or call the
Institute for further ordering information.

For Don Murray, whose spirit
stands behind everything we do.

About this series

SEPTEMBER 1990

The Poynter Institute for Media Studies proudly publishes the 12th volume of its series *Best Newspaper Writing*, valued since 1979 by students, teachers, and professionals as an indispensable text on clear, effective, and graceful newswriting.

As in past years, *Best Newspaper Writing* is a joint venture of the Institute and the American Society of Newspaper Editors. In 1978, ASNE made the improvement of newspaper writing one of its primary goals. The Society inaugurated a contest to select the best writing in several categories from newspapers in the United States and Canada, and to reward the winning writers with $1,000 prizes. (This amount was increased to $2,500 by the 1989 ASNE Writing Committee.) The Institute volunteered to spread the gospel of good writing by publishing the winning entries along with notes, commentaries, and interviews. That first volume, *Best Newspaper Writing 1979,* sold out long ago and has become a collector's item.

This year's volume is dedicated to Donald Murray, Pulitzer Prize-winning editorial writer at *The Boston Globe*, author of influential books on the teaching of writing, pioneering composition teacher and newspaper writing coach, and longtime visiting lecturer, consultant, and friend of The Poynter Institute.

Each spring a panel of ASNE editors meets in St. Petersburg for two days to screen more than 500 entries and choose the winners. The first six volumes of *Best Newspaper Writing* were edited by Dr. Roy Peter Clark, now dean of the faculty at The Poynter Institute.

Don Fry, an associate of the Institute and director of Poynter writing programs, co-edited the 1985 volume with Clark. Fry then took over the series from 1986 to 1989, adding the annual bibliogra-

phies compiled by Poynter's Chief Librarian Jo A.
Cates. This year, Fry is joined as co-editor by his
Poynter colleague, Dr. Karen F. Brown, who holds
degrees from Michigan State, Tennessee State,
and the University of Tennessee, and who has
taught at Poynter since 1986. Previously, she was
on the mass communications faculties of the University of Tennessee and the University of South
Florida, and was a reporter for the *Nashville Banner, Macon Telegraph and News,* and the *St.
Petersburg Times.* Brown will assume sole editor-
ship with the 1991 volume.

The 1990 award categories were deadline writing, non-deadline writing, commentary, editorial
writing, and state and local government reporting.
A committee of 16 editors, chaired by John S. Dris-
coll, editor of *The Boston Globe,* judged this year's
entries:

Christian Anderson, *The Orange County Register*
Richard Aregood, *Philadelphia Daily News*
Joann Byrd, *Everett* (Wash.) *Herald*
Judith Clabes, *The Kentucky Post*
Linda Cunningham, *Parsippany* (N.J.) *Daily
    Record*
Earl Foell, *The Christian Science Monitor*
Ellen Goodman, *The Boston Globe*
William Hilliard, *The Oregonian,* Portland, Ore.
Karen Jurgensen, *USA Today*
Saundra E. Keyes, *Philadelphia Daily News*
Bill Kovach, Nieman Foundation
Don Marsh, *Charleston* (W. Va.) *Gazette*
Jean Otto, *Rocky Mountain News,* Denver, Colo.
C. Michael Pride, *Concord* (N.H.) *Monitor*
Frank Sutherland, *The Times,* Shreveport, La.

The Institute wishes to thank these judges for their
fine work, and to compliment them for their dedi-
cation to good writing.

* * *

Founded in 1975 by the late Nelson Poynter,
chairman of the *St. Petersburg Times* and its Washington affiliate, *Congressional Quarterly,* the Institute was bequeathed Poynter's controlling stock in
the Times Publishing Company in 1978. It invests

its dividends in educational activities in four areas of print and broadcast journalism: writing, graphics, management, and ethics. The faculty teaches beginning and mid-career professionals, publishes teaching tools such as this book, and conducts educational and research projects, all of which seek the same goal: to raise levels of excellence in newspapers and the communications media generally.

The Institute congratulates the winners and finalists of the ASNE Distinguished Writing Awards.

Robert J. Haiman, President
The Poynter Institute

Acknowledgments

The *Anchorage Daily News* and Charles Wohlforth
The Boston Globe and Wil Haygood
The *Chicago Tribune* and Linnet Myers
The *Fort Lauderdale News/Sun-Sentinel* and Tom Kelly
The Hartford Courant and Mark Pazniokas
The *Mail Tribune*, Medford, Ore., and Terrie Claflin
The Miami Herald and David Von Drehle
The Orange County Register and Diana Griego Erwin
The Times Herald-Record, Middletown, N.Y., and
    Mike Levine
The Washington Times and Samuel Francis

We wish to thank the following people for their generous assistance in producing this volume: Jo Cates, Roy Peter Clark, and Joyce Olson of the Institute staff, editorial assistant Lisa Compton, and of course, the authors and their editors. Except for photographs and artwork, *Best Newspaper Writing 1990* was produced entirely on a Macintosh II computer and typeset on a Linotronic 300.

Cover art from a woodcut by Carlos Llerena Aguirre
Portraits by Rossie Newson
Book design and production by Billie M. Keirstead

Contents

Introduction

Most reporters write for the desk. Beginners quickly figure out what their editors will reject, change, butcher, get angry about, or pass through untouched. So they write defensively, taking the safest path to avoid blame and hassle.

Some reporters do not write for the desk, but for the reader. They reject the dulling tendencies of their safety-minded colleagues. They deliberately take risks, and enjoy the view from the high wire.

This year's winners of the ASNE Distinguished Writing Awards belong to the adventurous group. They take chances on tricky subjects likely to frighten their superiors, they write in ways that challenge our inherited tradition of flat and bloodless prose, and they stretch the imagination of our profession.

DAVID VON DREHLE

David Von Drehle of *The Miami Herald* risked his life for the story that won the deadline prize. Von Drehle and photographer Jon Kral deliberately reported Hurricane Hugo from inside the eye. They took shelter in the stairwell of a Sheraton hotel as the storm screamed overhead. Von Drehle portrays the hurricane as an unseen monster trying to get at him:

> ...At the bottom of one stairwell, we watch as the sucking wind tries to wrench open a double-bolted fire door.
>
> First the air yanks, then slips its fingers into the tiny gap between door and door frame, then strains at the heavy steel structure until the door actually *bends*.

As he sat on the stairwell steps, jotting down notes, Von Drehle watched the cinderblock walls moving beside him.

Besides his physical courage, Von Drehle took chances with the literary form of his account, writing in chronological order, the present tense, and the first person, all rare or taboo in newswriting. In the passage above, these three techniques, used in combination, put readers right into the scene, where the unseen storm-monster grasps at *them.*

Not only did Von Drehle calmly jot down notes as Hugo tried to get at him, he also played around with his style, a fact he dropped casually in his interview with Don Fry:

VON DREHLE: ...I've always felt that analogies were a weak spot in my writing. So...I looked on this story as a chance to try to work on that...

FRY: Now wait a minute! Are you telling me that you were experimenting with style in the middle of a hurricane?

VON DREHLE: Yeah. Yeah. I was.... Analogies don't just pop into my head, as they do for some good writers I know... And the only time I ever get an analogy at all is if I concentrate intently on what is happening, and laboriously go through the catalog of my other experiences to find something it matches. And so it occurred to me that this would be the opportunity to try that out.

What cool.

SAMUEL FRANCIS

Sam Francis took considerable political risks as he won the prize for editorial writing. The only person to win an ASNE award two years in a row, Francis serves as deputy editorial page editor for *The Washington Times,* the American right wing's flagship newspaper. But his position did not deter him from writing a scathing attack on the sexual hypocrisy of conservatives, including an editor for his own paper. Francis responded to a series of sexual scandals involving Democrats and Republicans alike, culminating in the 10-year suspended sentence for sexual battery for Quentin C. Crommelin, who served on the staffs of four prominent conservative senators:

Of course, none of these scandals on the right proves that conservatives "are just as bad" as liberals, or vice versa. What it does prove is that human nature is the same, regardless of which side of the political fence it favors. But many conservatives seem reluctant to acknowledge this, and few have come forward to denounce the mote in their own side's eye.

This week columnist John Lofton of *The Washington Times* interviewed Mr. Helms about the Crommelin case, and to his credit, Mr. Helms forthrightly read Crommelin out of his precincts. "I find this guy repulsive.... I have no use for him." But two of Mr. Helms's close advisers, Tom Ellis and Carter Wren of the National Congressional Club, were far more circumspect, as are many of Crommelin's associates on the right. "I viewed it as normal behavior of an active bachelor," says one of Crommelin's buddies on Foreign Relations. "I don't have the facts at this point," says Mr. Wren.

But the world and the court have the facts, and if conservative leaders pretend they don't see them, the world will judge them less mercifully than the court judged Crommelin. If conservatives, whose political agenda includes respect for the simple virtues of the Judeo-Christian tradition, don't treat the crooks and perverts among them at least as uncompromisingly as they treat Mr. Kennedy and Mr. Wright, that judgment will be to laugh them out of office as hypocrites and opportunists who haven't earned the right to be taken seriously.

Francis uses phrases like "crooks and perverts," "lurid stories of sexual harassment, violence, and rape," and "had their political lamps put out by floundering in sexual swamps of their own making." He finishes off the wounded on his own side.

LINNET MYERS

Linnet Myers of the *Chicago Tribune* won the
government reporting prize for a three-part series on
felony courts in her city. For 2-1/2 years on the court
beat, Myers never blinked, going so far as to devise
this ironic set of "rules":

With time, you begin to learn the rules of
the Criminal Court. Some are rules of law
and evidence. Others are unwritten rules.

There's the Criminal Court rule of motherhood: Mothers will lie for their children. A
mother will swear to tell the truth and then
testify that her son was with her, when he
was in fact committing murder.

A mother will stand up for her son—unless he was a baby and was beaten to death
by her husband or boyfriend. Then it is likely
that the mother will be loyal to her lover, not
to her dead son.

There are rules that say it's hard to get a
murder conviction for a child-abuse killing,
because the grown-ups often say they were
"disciplining" the children and didn't mean
to kill.

There are rules that say little children who
are sexually assaulted better be old enough not
only to say what happened but also to know
what day it is, what time it is, what truth is,
what a lie is. Because they have to prove they're
"competent" before they can even testify.

Other rules say the rape of a woman deserves the same punishment as the sale of 15
grams of cocaine. Rules say a rapist can get
out of prison and rape again—and again—
before he is put away for good....

Rules say the murder of a "dirty victim"—
like a gang member or a vagrant—isn't good,
but it's not as bad as the murder of a "clean
victim." Rules say there's no sexism, but it's
easier to get off if you're a woman.

Rules say there's no racism, but if you want
to escape the death penalty, *statistics indicate*

it's probably better to murder a black person than a white person.

Myers's editors added the gratuitous attribution "statistics indicate" in that last sentence.

Myers sets aside the usual cool of journalists to make a point about the emotional toll of reporting parades of human misery for too long. She draws on her own emotions, addressing the reader in the second person:

> There also are moments of shame, when injustice is done....
> You watch as Bennie Williams, a black man, gets the death penalty for killing a young-ster to steal his radio.
> Then you watch as Charles Hattery, a white man, is spared the death penalty even though he systematically murdered a mother—a black woman—and her two children.
> You find yourself glaring at the jurors, fu-rious, wondering, is this justice? And you wonder why you have become so angry at the thought that someone will not die.

Myers left the court beat, and wrote these sto-ries in the relative calm of features.

DIANA GRIEGO ERWIN

Diana Griego Erwin won a Pulitzer Prize for *The Denver Post* six months after she began as a journalist, and she won the ASNE commentary prize for her second column ever. The first Hispanic winner of this award, Erwin writes for *The Orange County Register,* mostly describing people far re-moved from the experience of mainstream readers.

She risks the displeasure of readers who have grown tired of hearing about American citizens crip-pled by their inability to speak English. In this scene, impatient clerks have rebuffed a frustrated Spanish speaker in the Department of Motor Vehicles:

> I watched as he leaned against a wall where

about 15 men waited. Many wore work pants and that same face, deeply lined from too much sun and too many worries.

I asked Luis Manuel Delgado why he waited.

"The lady who speaks Spanish has gone to lunch," he said.

There was no irritation in his voice, no anger at the time wasted. It was simply a fact.

I pointed out that the clerks hadn't treated him very nicely. Didn't that anger him? I wondered.

"I should know how to speak English," he said with a quiet simplicity. "This is the United States."

Later, Mr. Delgado gets his revenge, as Erwin gives him the last word in the column:

I asked him if it didn't hurt, being treated *como un burro*, like he said.

"No, I am not a donkey and my children know it. They know I do all this for them. They are proud of me. Nothing anyone else says or does can make me sad when they have pride in me.

"And they will never be donkeys."

He nodded toward the stressed-out information clerks busily shuffling papers behind the government-issued desk. "And they won't work here," he said. "This is donkey work."

Not content merely to observe the passing absurdities of Southern California snobbery and racism, Erwin sometimes engineers a scene of her own just to write a column about it, as she describes in Don Fry's interview with her:

ERWIN: ...this last Friday, President Bush was here in town speaking about drugs. And we covered it as a newspaper would and should. We covered the speech, and there were a lot of schoolchildren invited, so we interviewed kids. And I thought, "Well, this is preaching to the choir." So I found a couple of drug dealers and took them to the speech at the stadium...

FRY: You did?! [Laughter]

ERWIN: ...because I thought, "Well, these are the people who really need to hear this. And I would like to know what they think about this."

They liked it, although one of them said he found it "heavy."

TERRIE CLAFLIN

Terrie Claflin of the Medford, Oregon, *Mail Tribune* won the non-deadline prize for a five-part series that turns a number of stereotypes upside down. Anyone can write well about a crack baby, but few reporters would have the nerve to subvert the reader's presupposition that crack babies would be black and deformed. Claflin leads her series like this:

> She is, in many ways, a china doll. Skin like snow, eyes like sky, a tiny body rigid and cool to the touch. Her cheeks are rosy, her face expressionless, unchanging. The world swirls in color and motion around her, yet she does not perceive it. For like a china doll, within her tiny head, behind those ice blue eyes, Rachel has no brain.
>
> Rachel was born Jan. 2, 1989, at a hospital here in southern Oregon. The birth was premature, only three weeks before the due date, but there were severe complications apparently caused by the mother's drug use. The placenta had detached from the uterine wall. The baby was without oxygen for God-only-knows how long.
>
> God only knows how, or why, she lived. It wasn't until days later that computerized tomography scans showed that the baby's seizures and strokes were so intense inside the womb that most of her brain tissue had turned to a watery consistency.

The series focuses on Rachel and on Carole White, her foster mother, who knows that the baby will die soon. Since the stories would logically end with the baby's death, Claflin arranged ways for Carole to notify her so she could be present, as she tells us in her interview with Karen Brown:

CLAFLIN: ...I began leaving numbers of where I might be able to be reached over the weekend in case she took this dramatic turn for the worse, because we thought that we would want to be there and watch this all happen.... I could have been present at the death. They called me about 3:00 and the baby died about 5:00. They called me and I said that, at this point, I thought that it was a very private time for Carole and her family, and I was not going to subject them to photographs or me taking notes in the corner. I had said my goodbyes the day before to this baby, and at this point, I would let them grieve alone.

We think of journalistic risk in terms of aggressiveness, but sometimes courage takes the form of restraint.

* * *

Any journalist who reads these stories and the winners' interviews will have new models to imitate. Reporters may continue to write for the desk, and editors may continue to intimidate their writers into dullness, but these winners show us that it doesn't have to stay that way.

Karen Brown
Don Fry

BEST NEWSPAPER WRITING
1990

Terrie Claflin
Non-Deadline Writing

TERRIE CLAFLIN earned her bachelor's degree in speech communications from Southern Oregon State College and started working for the Medford *Mail Tribune* when she graduated in 1979. Along the way she spent a summer in Germany, and later received a scholarship to study political science at the University of Constance in West Germany. She and her husband spent 14 months traveling in Europe and talking with the people. Her interest in people continued as she returned to the *Mail Tribune* and moved from news reporting to writing features in the paper's Life section. The *Mail Tribune,* an evening publication owned by the Ottaway Newspaper chain, has a circulation of about 30,000.

Mother's drug habit turns baby into victim

JULY 19, 1989

She is, in many ways, a china doll. Skin like snow, eyes like sky, a tiny body rigid and cool to the touch. Her cheeks are rosy, her face expressionless, unchanging. The world swirls in color and motion around her, yet she does not perceive it. For like a china doll, within her tiny head, behind those ice-blue eyes, Rachel has no brain.

Rachel was born Jan. 2, 1989, at a hospital here in southern Oregon. The birth was premature, only three weeks before the due date, but there were severe complications apparently caused by the mother's drug use. The placenta had detached from the uterine wall. The baby was without oxygen for God-only-knows how long.

God only knows how, or why, she lived. It wasn't until days later that computerized tomography scans showed that the baby's seizures and strokes were so intense inside the womb that most of her brain tissue had turned to a watery consistency.

There was nothing the doctors could do. They kept Rachel in the pediatric unit at Rogue Valley Medical Center for a month before they decided she might be better off at home. The baby needed a mother who could rock and hold and comfort her 24 hours a day, if that's what it took. Rachel's own mother, however, wouldn't do.

For one thing, she lived too far from the pediatric center and the specialized care the baby would need. For another, before Rachel's mother left the hospital, both she and the baby tested positive for marijuana metabolites, amphetamines, and cocaine.

* * *

Carole White, a foster care provider, holds the baby in her lap, rubbing the fuzzy blond head, wrapping the tiny fingers around her own.

"I've picked up a lot of babies from the hospital, but I think they (hospital workers) were more upset about this one than I've ever seen before," she says.

Maybe it's because she's so beautiful, Carole says. And maybe it's because Rachel is going to die.

Rachel seems perfect, but at 6 months, she's so tiny. Rachel weighs only 9 pounds. She looks and acts like a newborn, spending most of her hours eating or sleeping. When she's awake, she either cries or looks blank, confused. She never smiles. She can see images and hear certain sounds, but can't make sense of it all.

Rachel's brainstem keeps her heart thump-thumping under her little flannel pajamas, Carole says. It sends hunger signals to her belly. And it allows her to feel pain—and comfort.

"She definitely knows the difference between lying in her crib and being held," Carole says. "Let's just say we've spent many an hour right here in this rocking chair, watching the sun go down and then come back up again."

Carole is a foster care provider for the state Children's Services Division. Just as the doctors suspected, Rachel is a 24-hour-a day job. Since she came home from the hospital in February, she has lost the ability to suck, so Carole has to feed her formula and sedatives every few hours with a syringe. The baby has frequent seizures—arching her back and contorting her body, howling and gasping for breath. Carole says that even Rachel's sleep is less restful than it was.

She changes every day, seldom for the better.

"Actually, she's doing pretty well, considering. They didn't think she'd live four months," Carole says, looking at the sleeping baby in her lap. "We're proving them wrong, though, aren't we Rachel?"

* * *

Carole and her husband, Charlie, live in a big farmhouse in the hills north of Central Point. The gate on the little picket fence out front has a latch on it, but it's seldom closed—not with all the comings and goings.

The Whites' two oldest children, Jon and Tracy,

are married, but they spend almost as much time here as they do at their own homes. The youngest daughter, Susan, is in high school, a cheerleader with friends and boyfriends who fill in whatever empty chairs might be found at the dinner table.

"I decided to start providing foster care when my son left home," Carole says. "I guess I was feeling a bit empty-nested."

That was four years ago. The family supported her decision, and six months later she was certified by CSD. She requested small children, not over the age of 5, and they began showing up regularly on her front porch, sometimes asleep on a police officer's shoulder, sometimes with nothing on but a T-shirt and diaper.

"I provide a place for children to go when their parents need some time to work out difficulties in their lives," Carole says. "It's usually short-term— sometimes for just a few hours. I bathe them and feed them and put them in sleeping bags on the floor."

More than 80 children have spent anywhere from a night to a couple of years with Carole and her family.

"These are children who are unbonded and lost," she says. "They don't seem to care that they are at a stranger's house. They just move right in. And we just make them part of the family. Even if we have them just for a night, I feel we can still make an impact on them. Maybe they'll know what's possible—they don't have to be beaten, they don't have to live in filth, they don't have to be hungry. We can show them that 'home' can be a secure place, that people can love one another, and that they are loved.

"The hardest part has been sending them home, wondering if their natural parents are going to take care of them the way I would...."

The hardest part got even harder two years ago. When Carole filled out her original foster care form with CSD, she said specifically that she did not want children with "special needs." Then came a little 11-month-old on a heart monitor. After that a baby addicted to heroin, then babies who were battered, babies who were neglected.

She took them all. Then, she decided she would take only kids with special needs. Rachel is the most recent.

"I guess sometimes you don't know yourself as well as you think you do," Carole says.

* * *

Violet has bright red hair and a way of crawling into just about anyone's lap. She is 3. She came to Carole's house when she was 7 months old—possibly the most severely battered child ever to survive at Rogue Valley Medical Center.

She would like to draw a picture, but she has trouble picking up a pencil. Two tries, three tries, and she has it between her stubby little fingers. She wrinkles her nose and grins. "I can do it."

Violet was born with fetal alcohol syndrome, caused by her mother's abuse of alcohol. She was beaten by her mother's boyfriend because he was tired of hearing her cry. She has had so many brain surgeries and come close to dying so many times that Carole has lost count. The CT scans show that large parts of her brain have died, and doctors are still unsure how that will affect the rest of her life.

While Violet has problems with speech and fine motor movement, Crystal appears to be a perfectly normal, curious, hey-look-out-world 4-year-old. She was never battered, Carole says, but she was neglected.

When Crystal arrived at the Whites' house at age 16 months, she crawled around looking for crumbs of food under the furniture. She couldn't speak and wouldn't look at Carole no matter how hard Carole tried to reach her.

It took months, but finally the love came back. Eventually, both of the girls were declared well enough to be adopted. So that's what Carole did— she adopted them herself.

"I had worked so hard building up a trust in them," she says. "How could I give them away?"

* * *

Carole would have adopted J.J. too, if she could

have. She walks to the bookshelf and picks up a photo album, its cover showing a baby boy with light blond hair, and eyes and a smile that seem to go in two different directions at once.

J.J. was a heroin baby. He cried 24 hours a day for three months. The drugs had left him blind in one eye and severely retarded. He wasn't supposed to live, but Carole says she willed him to anyway. In the next 2-1/2 years she willed him to feed himself, walk, run, laugh, and learn sign language.

He was doing well in February when Carole agreed to care for Rachel, to rock the baby until she died.

Then one night last March, J.J. died in his crib.

The baby who had been given a new lease on life was dead. The baby that was supposed to die, Rachel, was still alive.

The doctors said J.J.'s death was somehow linked to the heroin his mother had taken before he was born, but no explanation could soften the shock for Carole and her family.

With renewed determination, Carole began willing Rachel to live.

Observations and questions

1) Terrie Claflin said this story works in part because Rachel is not what people expect in a crack baby. Notice how many things we learn about Rachel from the lead. In what ways does the lead counter preconceptions about the babies of drug users?

2) The early drafts of this story didn't mention the mother's drug use until the fifth paragraph. Editors moved it to the second paragraph. Which is better, assuming that the headline didn't mention drugs? How do you decide when to lead with important information and when to delay it?

3) If the writer's intent was to delay the mention of drug use, what would a good headline say?

4) Count the characters who are mentioned in this part of the series, omitting Rachel and Carole. What do you know about each? Are there some who should have been left out? Is there additional information that you'd like about some characters?

5) Pick your favorite descriptive passage. Why does it work well? Consider sentence structures and word choices.

6) We're not told about J.J. until the last seven paragraphs of the story. What would be some other ways of presenting him in the story? What are the advantages and disadvantages of other approaches? What is the effect of ending with the section on J.J.?

7) This story tells of a truly unusual woman who took on four children in need of intense care. Carole and her family could have been presented as saints, yet Claflin gives us the feel of real people in a very tough role. How was Claflin able to achieve that? What are some of the common touches that emerge in the story?

Foster mom struggles to cope

SEPTEMBER 18, 1989

"I didn't want to do it, really I didn't. I wanted to keep things as normal as possible, as long as I could. I just wanted to do what's best for Rachel."

Carole White sits in a softly lighted room in Rogue Valley Medical Center's pediatric ward. She rubs the dark circles under her eyes.

"Putting the feeding tube down her nose will be easier for her—and for me as well," she says.

The tiny cocaine baby had taken a turn for the worse.

August is still a blur in Carole's weary mind. The baby began having seizures over and over again, crying and contorting for three long, awful weeks. Carole refused to sleep. Her 17-year-old daughter, Susan, began noticing that Carole couldn't complete a sentence anymore. A therapist who comes to the house and works with Carole's 3-year-old adopted daughter, Violet, contacted Children's Services and suggested that Carole take a vacation with her family.

She did, reluctantly, leaving Rachel with a respite care volunteer. The family went to Disneyland—and came back a week early. Carole just felt that Rachel needed her.

Now the seizures are under control; the baby is on an almost adult-level dosage of Phenobarbital, a sedative. But she's having trouble breathing. And she's lost the ability to swallow. Over the weekend Carole had to resort to an eyedropper to get any formula down her. She brought Rachel here to the hospital two days ago.

Medical staffers inserted the feeding tube, which drips baby formula from an IV unit, but not without much discussion, Carole says. How far can they, or should they, go to keep this baby alive?

The room is quiet. Crystal, Carole's other adopted daughter, watches cartoons from a chair in the corner. The nurses hustle in and out with charts and hushed words of encouragement. They have just replaced the tube and Rachel's newbornlike squalls have turned to sobs.

Carole rocks, endlessly, in a well-worn recliner. She manages a smile as Rachel opens her eyes.

"Are you going to be all right now?"

SEPTEMBER 27, 1989

Carole needed a friend—someone who understood what she was going through. Someone who wouldn't ask "why" she chose to take care of this baby. She has found that kind of friend in Christina Smith.

Christina is a respite care volunteer for Easter Seals. Every third night she takes Rachel to her home, a few miles away in Medford, so that Carole can get one good night of sleep a week and do some of the things she used to do with her family —such as go to high school football games to watch her Susan cheer, or go out to dinner with her husband, Charlie.

Rachel and her condition are no shock to Christina. If anything, the baby is a bright spot in her life.

Two years ago Christina's mother-in-law had a series of strokes and had to move in with Christina and her husband. Like Rachel, she was a round-the-clock commitment. Like Carole, Christina had no one to turn to.

"I know how desperate you get for some kind of respite," she says. "So this has become a special ministry to me. When I went through the hurt and anger of not having help, I knew I needed to do this."

The two women talk a lot on the phone. They laugh as much as they cry. This morning at 3 a.m., Christina called Carole in panic, afraid Rachel was about to die.

"She was just coughing so hard, she turned so limp, so blue, I thought I'd lost her," Christina says.

They took Rachel to the medical center, where

the doctors determined that the convulsions stemmed from a crimp in the feeding tube. They also diagnosed a slight ear and sinus infection. They put Rachel on antibiotics, replaced the tube, and sent her home.

Lying in her crib, Rachel is carefully propped on Boris the Bear, a gift from the hospital's nurses. She looks as if she's doing better. The tube has helped her gain a few pounds. Her color is pink, her body no longer rigid. The warm and snuggly position on the bear helps her breathe. She sleeps peacefully as Christina and Carole talk about their lives and the fragile life in the crib.

"People react so differently to this baby—she touches them somehow," Christina says. "Sometimes there are tears or anger. Sometimes they have no compassion at all."

Carole tells about an encounter she had in a fast-food restaurant last week. She and Crystal and Violet, plus a 4-year-old autistic foster care child who lives with the Whites, had been at the hospital all morning and needed lunch.

Carole put Rachel in her special infant seat and set her near the table. A woman eating nearby came over, saying rather loudly that the baby was obviously very sick and Carole had no business bringing her there.

"It happens more often than I wish," Carole says. "People don't want to deal with it. They say it's just too hard. They couldn't do it. They think maybe these children should be put away in a nursing home.

"And it's NOT easy. But it IS easy. It's not easy because we might lose her and we love her so much. But it IS easy because we love her so much."

Carole's lap is just big enough for the three children who are trying to climb into it. But if another was to come along, somehow she'd find room.

"These are special children; they have a glow about them that so-called normal children don't have," she says. "There's potential here. There's a message for all of us here."

It's a message both painful and promising,

Christina says. Take one of them in your arms. Hold her close. You'll feel it.

"She makes you feel so special, like you're holding a gift from God."

Observations and questions

1) Claflin starts the story in the present, gives a brief flashback, and returns to the present, all in the first seven paragraphs. What is the time period covered? What techniques and words move the reader through time?

2) Often quotations are used to advance a story. That's not the case in the first half of this piece, where few quotations are used. Notice the selection of quotations. What purpose do they serve? How does the writer advance the story without frequent quotations?

3) Near the end of the story Claflin says, "Carole's lap is just big enough for the three children who are trying to climb into it. But if another was to come along, somehow she'd find room." Consider the symbolism there. Attempt to use symbolism in telling a different section of this story.

4) Why is Christina important to the story?

5) The first part of the series introduces the facts on Rachel and Carole. What does this story add? What new facts do we learn? What are the moods and themes developed?

Loving hand guides infant during ordeal

OCTOBER 2, 1989

6 p.m.—Susan and Tracy are clink-clank-clearing the dinner dishes, Tracy's husband, Jon, is telling a story at the kitchen counter, Carole is mixing up a new bag of formula in the sink, Charlie is jangling his keys on the way out the door to a Camp Fire meeting, the three little kids are rolling and romping and wrestling on the living room floor.

A few feet away, Rachel sleeps through it all.

"We've tried everything," Carole says, measuring the formula and pouring it into the plastic pouch. "We thought maybe it was too quiet, so we left the radio on all night. We tried keeping her up all day and she ended up staying up for 49 straight hours.

"Nothing works. She still sleeps all day and stays up all night. That's just Rachel."

Susan says she's going to go get a movie. Carole suggests that it not be a tear-jerker. Not tonight. It's been a long day.

Rachel and Carole have been fighting a battle of body temperature all afternoon. Because Rachel has no brain, she has no thermostat. Her temperature can drop to 92 degrees in 20 minutes. If it gets down to 90, her systems will start shutting down.

The woodstove blazes in the middle of the room. A cat curls up under Rachel's crib. A little vase of roses withers on a table nearby. The heat is almost tropical. Most of the family runs around in shorts.

8 p.m.—Carole and Tracy set up a bathtub assembly line, plopping one kid in the tub, then passing him on to be dried and dressed, kissed and tucked under the covers. Violet has fallen asleep in a chair. As Tracy carries Violet upstairs, Carole sinks into her soft blue recliner. But before she can kick off her shoes, Rachel is stirring in the crib.

Carole shakes her head.

"Timing," she says.

9 p.m.—You can tell when Rachel is awake. Her breathing sounds like a drip-coffeemaker, gurgling, pop-popping, sniffing, fluids moving through airways, clogged. She starts to cry—long, soft, newbornlike waaaaaahs, followed by a cough, then an ooh-ooh-ooh and a pout. Carole picks her up, kisses her on the cheek, then lays the baby belly-down over her knees. With cupped hands she begins beating on the baby's back like a bongo drum.

"This is supposed to break loose the phlegm or whatever it is that's in there," Carole says, settling into a rhythm. "She likes it. She thinks it's fun."

Indeed, Rachel holds her head up high, eyes as wide as they've ever been. After a few minutes, she's quiet, alert. Happy.

11:45 p.m.—Having finished *Gorillas in the Mist*, a tear-jerker after all, most of the family and visiting friends have wandered home or to bed. Rachel sits in her infant seat, eyes half-open. Each breath comes hard. Tracy has one more lunch to pack before she pours another cup of coffee for her mom, softens the lights, turns down the TV, and disappears up the stairs.

"This has definitely disrupted my family," Carole admits. This summer the weeds in Carole's garden grew right alongside the vegetables. A lot of tomatoes never made it into jars, the camping equipment gathered dust in the garage. Besides the vacation to Disneyland, the family had a few outings—mostly without Carole. Because of Rachel's condition, Carole is afraid to get too far from home. Two nights out of every three she doesn't even get to sleep with Charlie. She usually just picks a place on the couch and takes short, restless naps. If she's lucky.

"You have to have a pretty strong marriage to do something like this," she says. "Even my mother doesn't understand. She thinks I'm putting myself and my family through too much by taking on this kind of commitment.

"I don't think I'm putting myself through too much."

But she does worry, out loud, about her family.

2 a.m.—The family has already been through one death this year: J.J.'s was a nightmare that came with no warning. Carole hopes that this time, this death will be better.

Doctors and nurses have told her that Rachel could die three different ways: She could have massive convulsions and not come out of them, she could get pneumonia and not recover, or she could slip into a coma and die in her sleep.

"The coma is definitely the easiest of the three," Carole says. "That's what we're praying for now. I've finally got it through my head that we're not going to save her. I finally understand and accept that."

Rachel is considered a "no code" with local emergency service agencies. That means that rescue workers are not to resuscitate her if she is in a life-threatening situation. She is not to be saved. Even the feeding tube was a question of possibly "going too far" to extend Rachel's life, Carole says.

Rachel coughs and cries and refuses to sleep.

"Look at her; she's not a happy baby. When she's awake, she's miserable. But someday," Carole says with a smile, "she'll be happy and whole and run and play. ..."

3 a.m.—The way Carole sees it, God has given her a chance to be a caretaker for these children while they are here on earth.

"Maybe that's arrogant for me to say, but I feel that's my job in life, my purpose," Carole says. "I feel, in my own way, I'm Rachel's caretaker and someday I'm going to hand her over to God."

Of course, some people would take one look at Rachel and wonder if there is a God at all. Why would He create this baby? Why would He put her, her real family, her foster family, her doctors, and her caseworkers through so much pain?

Carole shakes her head. She believes Rachel has her own purpose. It could be just to tell her story, to show people—in a painful, but powerful, way—what happens when pregnant women take drugs.

Or it could be to prepare Carole for the children yet to come. If the experts are right, if America sinks deeper and deeper into its drug problem, there will be many more Rachels for the Caroles of the world.

She would take another one in a minute. But she knows she can't take care of them all.

"There are so many children out there who need homes—not just foster care, but adoption," she says. "These are children with rough histories—babies from Medford, babies from our neighborhoods. Cocaine babies, heroin babies, battered children.

"But look at Crystal and Violet. I mean, they're coming out okay. If we had let the thought that Violet had permanent brain damage or that Crystal had been severely mentally abused...if we had let those things keep us from adopting them, think of the joy we would have missed."

Rachel yawns, a big yawn for such a tiny mouth, but her eyes refuse to close. The hands on the clock nudge closer to 4.

"If you really want to help, if you love kids, then there's no excuse," Carole says.

"Even Rachel. With all the hardships she's caused in our family—not being able to go anywhere, staying up all night, the fear that hurts so badly in your stomach when you think you're going to lose her—even with all that, she's such a blessing. After she's gone, that's what we'll remember."

4:30 a.m.—After a half-hour of seizures, Rachel's body finally relaxes. Her eyes close. Her breathing is peaceful, silent.

Carole adjusts the drip of the feeding unit, covers the baby with a blanket, and makes her way through the darkness to the couch.

5:30 a.m.—Tracy's husband, Jon, moves through the room on his way to his job at the mill.

6 a.m.—Charlie throws another log on the fire, grabs his lunch out of the refrigerator, and closes the door quietly behind him.

6:30 a.m.—Rachel is choking. Tracy, still in her pajamas, gropes in the darkness to pick Rachel up and hand her to Carole. The baby's breathing is fast, hard, loud, then muffled.

The house is silent.

At the bottom of the stairs, a soft pink shadow with a Cheshire Cat grin fades into view.

"Good morning!"

6:35 a.m.—Carole heads into the kitchen to make a fresh pot of coffee, hugging the tiny figure at her side.

"Good morning, Violet. Did you sleep well?"

Observations and questions

1) Too often journalists tell about what happens without showing readers what they see. Good writers seek ways to appeal to all the senses. What are the sensory appeals in Claflin's lead?

2) The first two paragraphs could have been collapsed into one sentence if Clafin had decided to tell us what was happening instead of showing us. Why is showing a better approach? How do the structures of the two paragraphs contribute to the point the writer is making? How can a writer with limited space take readers into a scene instead of summarizing what happened?

3) What do we learn about the White family in the first seven paragraphs? List what is stated and what is assumed.

4) Claflin said she learned that Rachel's body had no thermostat when she noticed the heat in the room while family members were wearing shorts. How can reporters learn to be more observant? How can they free themselves to ask questions even when the answer seems obvious?

5) Rachel can do little more than cry and move about a little, yet she is not presented as a living object devoid of personality. How does Claflin help us to see Rachel as a person?

6) What is the mood in the early morning hours at the Whites' house? What techniques help the writer convey that mood?

7) Reporters are taught to tell objectively what happens. In this story Claflin tells what she sees and what Carole says. Claflin also interprets Carole's thoughts and seems to raise some questions of her own. What are the advantages and disadvantages of her method?

Carole fights fatigue as Rachel weakens

OCTOBER 9, 1989

Carole could have gotten a night's sleep. But she couldn't sleep. Yesterday evening at 6, Rachel had a terrible spell. She coughed and gagged and turned purple. Charlie "whomped" her, as Carole puts it, until the baby started breathing again. Then she went to sleep.

"She's been gone ever since."

It's noon on Monday and Rachel is sleeping blissfully in Christina's arms. She's still the color of china, but her body acts as if it's made out of rags, limp, fingers uncurled, arms outstretched. Her tiny head is tucked in a little pink stocking cap. The face below it is puffed, blotched, unresponsive. Christina kisses her until there's a slight reaction—a yawn, a soft cry, a flutter of eyelashes.

Then she's gone again.

"It's a blessing," Carole says. "This is the way we hoped she would go, but now that it's happening, it's happening too fast."

Nancy Gish knocks on the front door, but no one hears it. She comes in anyway, as she has so many times before, carrying a country doctor's black bag with a city doctor's beeper attached to it.

Nancy is a nurse for the home health program at Rogue Valley Medical Center. She was working in the neonatal intensive care unit 10 months ago when Rachel was there. Now it's her job to continue providing that care, that comfort, from the office within her car.

"Rachel was such a beautiful baby; I remember her well," Nancy says. "But within 24 hours, you could tell there was something different about her. You'd look in her eyes and there was nothing there.

"Nothing."

She holds the baby in her lap, taking a temperature reading, listening with her stethoscope to the short, sharp breaths. As the canary in the corner starts to sing, Rachel's eyes open. Then they close again.

"It certainly looks like a semicomatose state to me," Nancy says, gently. Carole asks the nurse what will come next and Nancy explains that more than likely, Rachel's systems will start to shut down. A damaged brain simply lacks the capacity to keep things working the way they should.

As that happens, Rachel will become more lethargic, her heart will speed up and then start slowing down.

"She's going to sound worse, but it will be easier on her," Nancy says. "That's what we're hoping for."

Nancy stops to dab at a tear with her finger and smiles at the baby.

"Are you getting at peace with everything?" she asks softly. "Is that what's happening?"

OCTOBER 11, 1989

Carole debated whether it was too early to buy Rachel a new dress, her last dress, and a little band with a bow to put around her head. She decided it wasn't.

"I just felt like it was too soon—like I'd be rushing things to start making her final arrangements," Carole says as matter-of-factly as she can. "But everyone says it will be easier if I do. So I am."

Today Rachel has an appointment with her pediatrician, Alan Frierson. Carole knows that there's not much he can do, but she still wants to know what he thinks about Rachel's new condition.

They undress her except for the little white bow stuck to her thin blond hair, weigh her (14 pounds), and wrap her up in blankets while they wait for the doctor. He arrives, does a quick exam, and asks that everyone else leave the room so he can talk to Carole.

Out in the waiting room, mothers wait with their healthy babies—babies that kick and coo and toss their rattles and think and feel and respond.

When Carole finally emerges from the office her

jaw is set, her brown eyes sharp and round.

"Do you want to know what he told me? He told me that despite what everyone else says, he doesn't think we're dealing with a dying baby. He says she may just be slipping into a 'happy sleep.' That she may be this way for 20 years."

With Tracy's help, Carole carries the baby out to the car, buckles Crystal into the back seat, then stands in the parking lot with empty hands.

"In a way, I'm relieved; in another way, I'm disappointed," Carole says, looking up at the sky. "I know that sounds awful. I hope you understand. It's just not fair to Rachel."

She had planned to make the funeral arrangements tomorrow.

"I'm just so incredibly confused..."

* * *

Dr. Alan Frierson is a long, lanky man with the thought pattern of a pinball machine. His ideas bounce off the top of his head and ricochet around the room, seemingly faster than he can say them.

One idea stands firm.

"I absolutely think Rachel is going to be 40 years old someday, lying somewhere in a nursing home unable to move and unable to speak," he says sadly. "(What is left of) her brain has kept her alive this long; it should be easier to stay alive all the time."

As she ages, the airways will get bigger, making it easier to breathe. The organs will mature. Her body will set itself on automatic pilot. There will be no one visible at the controls.

"My biggest problem is burning out Carole. She's a valuable resource for Medford and I'd hate to lose her," Frierson says.

OCTOBER 13, 1989

You can only balance on an ethical tightrope so long. After a while, you either fall or jump. Today Carole has decided to jump. She's weighed the professional opinions in one hand with her gut feeling in the other—and made an appointment at Conger-Morris Funeral Directors for 2 p.m.

"Wednesday (the day of the doctor's appointment) was the hardest day yet," she says. "I was devastated. And then I was so guilty for feeling devastated. How could hope make me feel so bad?"

Rachel is dressed in soft pink pajamas. She gurgles in Christina's lap as the funeral director, Chuck Loyd, goes over the details. He remembers Carole from J.J.'s death seven months ago, so he skips most of the paperwork.

The state will provide $304 for the burial. But whatever Carole wants, Conger-Morris is willing to make up the difference. A marker on the gravesite will cost at least $300 more. Carole says it will be marked one way or another.

Loyd is curious about the baby. He asks questions, delicately, which Carole answers, honestly. She tells him the whole story, right up to her decision to make these arrangements.

"I think an animal is an animal. We've raised rabbits and sometimes these baby rabbits are born and they don't do very well and I'd work and work and try to save them." Carole fingers the chair. "She reminds me of these baby rabbits. No matter what I do, she's going to die."

OCTOBER 17, 1989

Steven Morris of Conger-Morris calls and offers to pay for the gravesite marker. Carole wonders aloud how one tiny baby can have such a big impact on so many hearts. Rachel is sleeping well, she says. It's a good day.

OCTOBER 27, 1989

Rachel was in a complete coma for 14 hours four days ago. She's come out of it, but she hasn't been the same since. She's not tolerating her feedings well, her diapers are dry as if nothing is going through, and she has serious problems breathing when she is awake. The day after she came out of the coma, she stopped breathing. Carole says she panicked, and revived Rachel.

"Not yet," she says. "It's not right yet."

Carole says she catches herself wishing, sometimes, that Rachel would drop back into the coma. Then it would be easier. Then they could talk about stopping her feedings. But then, Rachel and God have their own plans, she says.

Carole has decided to keep Rachel at home and not send her to Christina's every third night as she has. Christina comes over and helps Carole catch an occasional nap, and tends to the baby so Carole can tend to her family.

While the baby sleeps bundled in her crib, Carole and her oldest daughter, Tracy, are cleaning house. The younger ones, Crystal and Violet, try to stay one step ahead of the vacuum, scattering crayons in their wake. Carole's husband, Charlie, and her youngest daughter, Susan, should be home soon. No one is sure what's for dinner. Carole looks out the window at the darkening clouds and laughs about this compelling urge she has to go out and walk in the rain. Without an umbrella.

That's what she used to do, back when she was younger, in high school, she says with a grin. She'd break up with a boyfriend or have some other major event happen in her life, and she'd step out into the rain and walk until she was drenched.

When she got back, everything would be better.

Tracy shakes her head, grins, and goes back to helping the kids color.

Oh, by the way, Carole says, she and Christina found this wonderful saying that they want read at the funeral. It was on a coffee cup and Carole copied it down on a piece of lined paper. It says:

Some people come into lives and quickly go.
Some stay for a while and leave footprints on
    our hearts,
And we are never ever the same.

There is less sadness than joy in Carole's face.

"It says it, doesn't it? It says it all."

Observations and questions

1) This story is a balanced portrayal of day-to-day activities, medical tasks and terms, and the poignant sorrow of creeping death. What are some examples of each? How does the writer keep the balance? What would be the results of tipping the balance in any of the three directions?

2) In the middle of the article Claflin says: "They undress her except for the little white bow stuck to her thin blond hair, weigh her (14 pounds), and wrap her up in blankets while they wait for the doctor." What is the value of such details at this point in the story?

3) A standard journalism rule says the writer should stay out of the story. When Carole visits the doctor, however, it is clear that the writer was not allowed in, then has an important conversation with Carole when the visit ends. Does Claflin's method of letting Carole address her directly distract from the story? When should stories include direct address?

4) A key to good writing is selection of material. Consider three sections that might have been omitted: Dr. Frierson's discussion on Rachel's survival, Carole's quote about baby rabbits, and the passage on Carole's desire to walk in the rain. What would the story lose if any of the three had been deleted?

5) This story tells what we've known since the eighth paragraph of the first story: Rachel is going to die. Was this part of the series necessary? Consider the effect of going from part three to part five. What do we gain in part four?

Rachel: A final journey

NOVEMBER 12, 1989

Rachel died on Wednesday, just four days ago, at 5:34 p.m.

Carole was holding the baby in her arms, in the recliner where they had spent so many hours, when Rachel opened her eyes one last time, took a deep breath, let it out, and left the world, with all its pain and suffering, behind....

* * *

Oregon State Police officers met with District Attorney Bill Juba on Thursday morning to discuss possible prosecution of Rachel's mother. Upon handing over the case to the district attorney, Lt. Del Hussey said, "The OSP is behind it. We'd like to see it prosecuted and I have committed any resources I have available to get it prosecuted."

Juba said no decision had been made. The state has one year from the date of the "crime" to file charges. Since the damage to the infant occurred at birth, Jan. 2, 1989, a decision must be made by Jan. 1, 1990.

"We are still in the stages of investigation," Juba said, "not only in the investigation of this particular case, but from the entire legal perspective as well.

"No decision is forthcoming at this time."

* * *

Services for Rachel will be held at 11 a.m. Monday at the Conger-Morris Chapel in Central Point. Carole considered burying Rachel with Boris, the bear she snuggled with in her crib, but it is the only thing Carole has that was truly Rachel's. Instead, Carole plans to buy a new teddy bear to place in the casket "so she won't be alone."

An interment, at Memory Gardens, will be attended only by Carole and her family.

* * *

Rachel's mother, who declined to be interviewed for this special report, is due to have another baby in December.

Observations and questions

1) When Claflin and her editors planned this series, they didn't know whether Rachel would be alive or dead at the publication date. How would you have ended it if Rachel had lived in a coma?

2) Throughout the series Claflin excelled in transitions by phrasing the end of one paragraph to tie into the next. This story, however, is composed of four very different units with abrupt shifts between each. What is the effect? Why does it work well?

3) Legal implications and Rachel's mother were barely mentioned in the series. Should they have been a part of the conclusion? Would you have mentioned them more throughout?

4) We reach the end of the series before learning that Rachel's mother is one month away from having another baby. What is the effect? Would you have preferred to end the series with one of the earlier segments in this story?

5) People, including drug babies, are dying each day in this nation. What elements in this story are unique? Should there be more stories like this?

A conversation with
Terrie Claflin

KAREN BROWN: Tell me a little about Medford, Oregon. I'm the only one who doesn't know, but where is it?

TERRIE CLAFLIN: It's right on the border of Oregon and California. It's in a small valley, and most of the industry here is in timber and in fruit crops, particularly pears.

Most of the people here traditionally have been long-term families that settled in this area. But we are becoming a depository, so to speak, for a lot of people who are escaping from California, and for a lot of retirees who are looking to get out of the cities and to find more of a rural community.

I noticed that you received several writing awards prior to the ASNE award. What were some of the others?

I won two writing awards as well as three feature and investigative awards from the Oregon Newspaper Publishers Association. One story was on rain. We had gone through a particularly long dry spell, and one spring morning there came this wonderful shower. I watched everyone come out onto the porches and revel in it, and I wrote a piece called "The Return of the Rain."

And then the second time that I won, the story that stood out was called "Dirty Dancing." We had one of our very first topless bars come to Medford. Instead of reporting about the outrage of the community, which there definitely was, I decided to look at it from the dancers' perspective. I spent

EDITORS' NOTE: *We have edited these conversations heavily for clarity and brevity, and in some cases recomposed the questions.*

probably a month talking to these women, and watching them perform, and really kind of getting to know them, and what their reasons are for getting up there.

You have an offbeat approach to things. How did that come about?

I think that's probably from my original desire to write fiction and fantasy and science fiction. I just have a way of saying "what if?" and looking at the world as if things might be different.

Did you read a lot as a kid?

Uh-huh. I did read a lot, from day one, I think. I've always walked around with books in my hands and had them stashed next to the bed and everyplace else.

Were there books that stood out?

My favorite writer would have to be Ray Bradbury for his concepts, the way he uses words...simple words. I mean, he never gets very complex in the words that he chooses, but he comes across with these marvelous ways of presenting things. He's just such a wonderful wordsmith that he would have to be my favorite.

Okay. And that stood out in your piece: use of words and simple structures. Are there writers now, journalists, for whom you have a great deal of respect?

I don't think that I would pick out any one. I'm constantly amazed by what a lot of the bigger papers are doing, and the time and the energy they can put into some of these pieces, and the wonderful stories that result from them.

You talk about an offbeat approach to writing, yet one of the criticisms of journalism is that too often writers follow the same footprints. Do you

have criticisms about the way American journalism is going today?

I tend to think sometimes we forget the human aspect. You can write a lot of stories about how awful the problem is, but when you actually find someone who it affects, you can get that message across so much better by just focusing on what that one person goes through, and showing that the issue does make an impact on someone's life. That's the way I prefer to do my stories, from a real, intensely human standpoint.

In addition to writing feature stories, you write a fitness column.

Yeah. I have been doing that for about five years. I'm real interested in fitness and health and began writing so many life stories on that subject that the *Tribune* decided to make it a weekly feature in the sports section.

So what kind of things are in your column?

Everything from profiles of people who may be the last finishers in the race; instead of concentrating on the first people, I'll concentrate on who came in last. Or maybe someone who's made some major changes in life. I've done a story on a person who was a drug addict and found that running was the only thing that could take the place of the drugs. I've written on everything from cellulite to cholesterol, and your basic health information as well. I try to balance columns so that readers might learn about someone one week and then learn about a topic or issue the next.

And the sports department takes this well, having a feature writer contributing there?

Oh, yeah. They're happy with it.

You've been a staff feature writer since 1981?

Yes. However, I did have one change in that about four years ago I cut back to more of a part-time job. I had had a second child, and life was just too hectic. I worked out an arrangement with the *Tribune* so that I could work anywhere from 21 up to 40 hours just so I could maintain my family life as well.

How did that work? Was there much resistance, or is that something that's done by others there?

It was kind of a new arrangement, but there was another full-time reporter, a woman who also had two small children, who was feeling the same way, and so the *Tribune* decided to create a job-sharing position. She worked the beginning of the week, then I worked from Wednesday to Friday, and we'd overlap in the process. We both had computers at home so we did a lot of writing at home on our days off, as well.

I think news just drains you somehow. Those deadlines, and all of the enthusiasm and adrenaline that goes into news, at some point start taking a toll on your life, and you need a break.

Do you still file from home sometimes?

Yes, sometimes. You know how it is in a newsroom. It's pretty hectic around here trying to get anything done, especially when you're working on a sensitive story, or one that has required a lot of time and a lot of notes. It's easier for me to go home and lay notes out in the middle of my spare bedroom, go through them, and organize my thoughts. I leave my answering machine on.

Okay. Let's talk about the stories. How did you come up with the idea for this series?

The photo editor here at the *Mail Tribune,* Steve Johnson, had been looking for some kind of a long-term piece, something that we could put heart and soul into, oh, ever since he's been here. Probably about eight years.

I didn't realize that I'd found it, at first. One of our editors had overheard that there was a foster care provider in the area who was taking care of a cocaine baby, and the baby was terminal. That's all he heard. He mentioned it to me, and so I thought, "Well, I'll go out and talk to the woman and produce a feature for next week."

When I went out there and spent an afternoon with this woman, I was so taken by the situation, and by the baby, and by the commitment that she had to such an incredibly hard job, that I knew the story was going to be a lot more than I expected. And so as soon as I came back to the newsroom, I went immediately to the photo lab, and told Steve that I had found what we'd been looking for, that I'd found a project for us to really put heart and soul into.

Why did you want a project?

In a paper this small, there are so many times when you only get to do one or two interviews for a story, when you may only have a day or two days to put together a feature, and I really wished that I had more time, and I thought if I had a project that was worthy that the *Tribune* would support me on it and say, "Go ahead and take the time and see what you can do if you were to study a person for a length of time."

There have been many stories on drugs. What were your thoughts when you approached this about how it would stand out, how it wouldn't be the same old thing?

Well, I basically decided to focus in on Carole, the foster care provider, and the baby. That's where I was going to go with it from the very beginning. I was going to stick with them through...well, through the death, if it happened, or for several months, if it didn't. We didn't know if the baby would live for forty years, or if she'd die in four days.

Tell me the total time involved. The dates on the stories in the tabloid covered about five months,

July to November.

Right. That was about the same as the reporting and writing. The very first story in the tab is from the first interview I had with Carole in July.

What kind of consultation went on with your editors after you met Carole and Rachel for the first time?

Well actually, I didn't present it to my editors right away. I didn't have the legal permission to write about this baby. Carole talked to me off-the-record because I didn't have permission from the Children's Services Division, or from the baby's biological mother.

I was allowed to have a post office box number for the mother, and began sending letters to her almost once a week for about a month or so, and she never responded. And so at that point, I began getting sort of frustrated, and began trying to go a legal route. I went to my editor and showed him the pictures that we had taken so far, and he said, "Whatever it takes. Just do it right."

We met with the attorney to see what kind of stand I might be able to take to get legal permission. At that point, I began meeting with juvenile authorities, and...

Hold on. Let me go back a little bit. When you met with the editor, what were the things that you said that convinced him?

I think it was nice to have the pictures with me so that he could actually see that this baby was not deformed, and that what we had here was an incredible example of some serious damage by drugs in a child that otherwise would have been very normal. And it really brought the whole issue home.

Would it have mattered if the child had been deformed, if Rachel had not been as beautiful as she was?

Maybe when you say she didn't have a brain, you expect this baby to be terribly disfigured. And she wasn't. That was what was so striking about it. She was a beautiful baby, and she looked completely normal, except for somewhere, because of her mother's drug use, something inside snapped during one of the seizures, and basically the brain had disintegrated. I think that that conflict, between the way she looked and the way she was, had a lot of rich value in terms of telling the story.

Okay. Now, go ahead. So you showed it to the editor.

And we, at that point, began pursuing it from a legal standpoint. We went to the juvenile authorities, Children's Services Division, and a judge, before Children's Services made a state ruling on it. They decided that the story was important enough to go ahead and open the case file to me. This had never been done before without a biological mother's permission. But they said the one condition was that I change the name. So that's what we decided to do.

Oh, that's unusual. How were you able to convince them?

Well, I met with an official and presented my case to him. And he's so frustrated with the situation. Even though we're living in this small, rural community, and our problem may not seem as intense as living in Oakland, the drug situation is still here, and he...as he said he never went into this job thinking that he would have to deal with these problems.

He thought he was going to deal with kids that were out of control, or needed some guidance, but he had no idea he would be taking children away from battering situations and from drug-abusing situations. And he's so frustrated with the whole thing that he really supported the story, and said he'd do everything that he could.

And Rachel is not the baby's real name?

No. I call her Rachel, but it's with difficulty, because I called her by her real name for the whole time that we worked. We changed the name to Rachel about a week before the section came out. I just had to go through all of my stories and change the name. And that was a name that Carole had chosen. I wanted her to be comfortable with it as well.

Now, when you had the legal permission what happened?

Once we had that, we basically just dove into the story and began spending as much time as we could with Carole and the baby.

What does that mean? Did you know, at that time, that it would be a tab?

No, I...well, maybe I did. I knew it was no longer one story, because once you wrote the story about this child, people were going to think that she was just a unique case, and there was only one cocaine baby in the valley. That was the response from a lot of people when I mentioned the story. They said, "Oh, we have a cocaine baby in Medford."

In my studies and research, I had found that one child in 10 is affected by illegal drugs before birth, and that's as true here in Medford as it is anywhere in this country. Rachel was just one case, and an extreme case, but at the same time, one that really brought it home.

So I decided at that point that I needed to tell Rachel's story, and I knew it would be long, because if I spent months on this, there was no way I was going to condense this into a short version. Then I also had to explain these situations in statistics here in Medford, and in Oregon, and then how each of the social services was responding to the situation.

At that point, I approached John Reid, the paper's editor, and asked if we might make this a special news tab, and he supported me.

Your colleague throughout this had been the

photographer?

Right. The other person that eventually came into play here was our graphic designer, Garrett Miller. I also have a strong interest in graphics, so Steve, Garrett, and I worked on it together. And then at the end, we had a special sections editor, Steve Dieffenbacher, who began designing the individual pages following Garrett's example.

You mentioned something about "in your research." How did you approach the story in terms of readings and any other background?

When we were waiting to get some kind of permission to go with the story, I began trying to assemble as much background information as I could. I went to the library and tried to come up with any recent stories that had been done by any major newspaper or magazine on the topic, but it was really new. There had been short things by news magazines, and a newspaper had some of the best, most comprehensive stories that I was able to track down through the library.

But a lot of that information wasn't used in the tab eventually. It just provided a feel for how representative Rachel was of the problem.

I ended up buying a three-ring binder and dividing it into the various sections: statistics, the legal profession, the medical profession. Rachel's story was a division in there. I think I had about 10 to 12 divisions in the binder. Whenever I came across something that pertained, I would make a copy of it, punch holes in it, and file it in this binder. It was the first time I'd ever done that, and it was incredibly helpful. Rather than having all of these papers everywhere, stuffed in notes, I would transcribe my notes and put them in this binder.

That's awfully well-organized.

After four months, things do have a tendency to blur, especially those notes you took in the beginning. It was time consuming, but it's something I usually did on my day off at home, or in the evenings, while sitting with my family. I'd be going over my notes and reorganizing them, and figuring out where my gaps were. And now the binder itself is like gold to me.

Now, the approach to the White family. What was the conversation like the first time that you talked to them?

It was rather awkward. You've got someone with a dying baby in her arms, and you kind of wonder what kind of questions you can ask. Luckily, Carole was really honest and very open about the situation, and then as I was talking with her, I found out that she had lost another baby several months earlier that had been a heroin baby. It was incredible what she'd gone through, but she just talked it all out. She told me everything.

And this was during your first conversation?

Yes.

Okay, you've gotten the Whites' permission. They know you're doing this in-depth story. How did you manage to be with them and not interfere?

A lot of times it's a matter of leaving your notebook in your purse for the first 15 minutes or half-hour. I've found that that can be a real important technique for getting people to start talking to you, and confiding in you, before you bring that pencil and notebook out.

And then, as they're talking, there may be a point where you bring it out and set it in your lap. All the while, though, if they're saying something really important, you're trying to keep that quote or that information in your head. But I think that being patient, and showing them that you're not there to get absolutely every sentence, is important.

What about Steve? Was he usually there with you?

Yes. He spent as much time there as I did. He has three children, and so there were lots of times we pitched in and did what we could to help the family keep running and make things easier for Carole, because she was getting incredibly worn out by the process.

But he's a little more conspicuous. He's got a camera. Were there any special ways to blend in without being so conspicuous?

Well, a lot of times he'd shoot for 15, 20 minutes, put the camera down, and then just spend time with them, playing with the kids, or going in and helping himself to a cup of coffee and standing in the kitchen without his cameras on his arms until something happened, and then he'd race back in and get it.

Let's talk about how to write a long story. Did you have a plan? Did you write from an outline? You said you had the book of notes, but how do you write a story this long?

I thought I was going to write one story, and I thought I'd probably even begin with the death, I mean, that being the climax. But when I began looking at my notes, I began seeing this from a fiction writer's standpoint, where you've got to work your way into the story, and then provide someone with some reward at the end, or some reason for actually reading through that long of a story.

And so I began taking it chronologically. I just began with the first interview. That way, readers could kind of follow the clues as they went through to the end of the story, and find out for themselves whether she lived or died at the end.

The lead says: "She is, in many ways, a china doll. Skin like snow, eyes like sky, a tiny body rigid and cool to the touch. Her cheeks are rosy,

her face expressionless, unchanging. The world
swirls in color and motion around her, yet she
does not perceive it. For like a china doll, within
her tiny head, behind those ice-blue eyes, Rachel
has no brain."
How did you write the lead?

Actually, this was the second attempt that I had tak-
en at the lead. The first attempt was a much more
direct: "Rachel has no brain, period." It's the shock
element there. And I wrote that, and wrote the first
three or four graphs, and didn't like it. I walked
around for about two days, just trying to decide
what it was I didn't like about it, and the thing was
that it just didn't seem human enough. Just to say
that someone has no brain was just too powerful,
too inhuman, I guess, to be possible.

And so I began trying to describe her as being a
living organism, a living person, and then showing
that conflict between the way she looked and what
she was. I needed that to come out in the first graph.

**At the end of the second paragraph, you wrote:
"The baby was without oxygen for God-only-
knows how long." You repeated that phrase in
the beginning of the next paragraph.**

That's something that I do a lot. I see my writing as
a chain of individual links, and it's very hard to cut
my stories because the paragraphs do link so well.

**Can that be a defensive mechanism against edit-
ing?**

Possibly, yes.

Does it usually work well?

Uh-huh.

**In the third paragraph, you mention "tomogra-
phy scans." How do you talk about complex issues,
technical terms, without zonking out the reader?**

Well, I wanted to say "CT scan," because I think that that's what most people are familiar with. However, a lot of people don't know what a CT scan is either. They don't know what "CT" stands for. So we opted to go ahead and spell that out, but I didn't want to get completely involved in it, and have to explain what the procedure is. By saying what they showed, that "the baby's seizures and strokes were so intense inside the womb that most of her brain tissue had turned to a watery consistency," to me tells you what the scan did.

What about that last phrase there? "Most of her brain tissue had turned to a watery consistency." Is that your phrasing, or did you get that from someone else?

I got that from a doctor, the pediatrician. He had actually used the word "mush," but I didn't like that.

Did you have to draw that out of him, have him redefine and redefine, or how did that emerge?

No. I just basically asked what was in there. I mean, when you get the scan, is it just completely gone? Is there no brain there, or what was it? I had to ask direct questions to get that answer.

All right. You mentioned the mother earlier, but it was really in the fourth paragraph that you brought her in: "The baby needed a mother who could rock and hold and comfort her 24 hours a day, if that's what it took. Rachel's own mother, however, wouldn't do." And again you end with a very powerful statement. What were your obligations to the mother? You said you'd never talked to her?

No. She never responded to my letters.

She's a character in the play who's never really there. What thoughts did you expect the reader to have about her?

I had hoped that she would respond and give some defense, because in another story in the tabloid there were drug mothers who did talk about their lives. And you did really feel sorry for them when you heard the way they had grown up, and the decisions along the way, and their experiences that had led to the drug abuse problem.

And I had really hoped that the mother would go ahead and talk about her own situation, so people wouldn't see her as the villain in all of this. But she never did, and so I basically left her out. The fact that she produced the child, and had the drug problem at the time, were the only facts that I could use.

Then the story shifts to Carole White. You've discussed the series as Rachel's and Carole's story. Was either one the main character?

No. No, I think this is kind of a shared thing. The editors had actually thought that I was going to write a story about Rachel and then a sidebar about Carole, but the two were so intertwined, and you can only say so much about the baby. I mean, it's not as if you can ask questions and find out what it's like to be in there, or how this baby feels about all of this. There were no quotes. And the two lives were just so linked. Carole had just about given up a lot of her family duties in an effort to provide love for this baby, so that there was no way to break them apart.

I counted 21 characters in the story. How do you bring people forestage, then move them backstage, and keep the story moving without people tripping all over each other?

I try not to introduce too many people at once. As you notice, Rachel has her time, and the very first five graphs are hers, to introduce who she is. And then when you realize that the other mother, the biological mother, would not do in this case, that there had to be someone else, then Carole naturally stepped in.

I tried to keep a lot of the statistics and things lower. I have a tendency to keep ages and things like that further down in the story than do a lot of other reporters.

I tend to save some of those aspects about their character, and their statistics, and include them throughout the story, so it becomes a learning process for the reader.

By paragraph eight you had given further description of Rachel and you were building on the effect that she had on hospital workers. The paragraph reads: "Maybe it's because she's so beautiful, Carole says. And maybe it's because Rachel is going to die." I think that that's when the reader first learns that she's going to die. Tell me about the impact that you expect that sentence to have on the reader.

Well, a lot of them may have closed the paper and not read anymore. A lot of my friends have even called me, once they heard of the ASNE award, and said, "Gee, I was going to read your section, but I just didn't think I could take it. And would you please send me a copy now?" [Laughs]

I tend to think that for a lot of people, it scared them away from the story...or some people it did.

One person at the newspaper had said that he really didn't want his wife to read it, because he thought it would depress her. He was hoping to pull it out of the paper before she got it in the morning. So I think some people just didn't want to deal with it.

I'm concerned about reader abuse. You've got a story here that's truth the reader needs to know. Yet, how do you keep from abusing the reader?

Well, in the format that I chose to write the story, nobody really knows if she's going to die, or if she's not going to die, and it's just basically an honest window into this part of life.

I try not to depress them too soon, and I try to use some paragraphs, some scenes later in the story

42

that are a little more upbeat, that show that Carole is not just walking around grieving and depressed, that she accepts this as life, and that she's doing the best that she can, and she's going to love the child anyway. I hope that that warmth, that hope, kind of balance out the reality that she will eventually die.

So you were conscious of that as a way to help people make it through the very sad parts?

Yes, because as I began working on the story, I would talk with my husband about it, talk with my friends about it, and say, "Here's this story I'm working on," and I'd listen to their questions.
"Why would this woman do this? Why would she volunteer to do this? How could she possibly volunteer to accept a baby that she knows is going to die?" And so I had to get to those questions when I talked to Carole, and it took those four months to really get down to it. But the essence of it was that the baby needed love, no matter what the circumstances, and that Carole was going to give it. And that she felt that that was her assignment in life, and in that aspect of it, she was going to try to make the baby's life as wonderful as she could.

Are you saying that the reporting considered theoretical readers as it went along?

Yes.

Is that common for you?

Yes. I bounce a lot of ideas off my husband and friends in an effort to find out what they want to know about the story, because I'm sometimes too close to it. And as I listened to these questions, I would jot them down and make sure that my story answered them.

Well, did you also get on everybody's nerves?

Yes. They didn't want to hear about it, either.

Later you wrote: "'She definitely knows the difference between lying in her crib and being held,' Carole says. 'Let's just say we've spent many an hour right here in this rocking chair, watching the sun go down and then come back up again.'"

That was so beautiful, as compared to, say, "She sits up a lot of nights rocking the baby." How did you get the lively quotation?

Spending time. She said that probably three or four different ways in the course of four months, but the words were so much better that time. It's just spending time, and talking to someone as a friend instead of as a reporter.

Then, moving on: "'The hardest part has been sending them home, wondering if their natural parents are going to take care of them the way I would....'

"The hardest part got even harder two years ago...."

I like the writing there, the play on "the hardest part."

That's another one of those transitions that I work for.

Did those come out on first writing, or is that in the editing stage?

No, they came out on first writing. In fact, I very seldom go through and revise my work. I'm a writer who starts at the beginning, and if I am not happy with that paragraph, I will not go on to the next. The writing process itself is not necessarily easy for me.

The only way I can compare writing to anything else is, it's like sleeping in Kansas in August when the air conditioning is broken. I twist and I turn and I jump up, and I sit back down, and I open the window, and I go back to my seat, and I get a drink of water, and then I sit back down, and it's just an incredible restless process for me.

It's painful to me. Every story I write tends to be

that way...or a lot of them. But it's worth it, when you get done, and you read the paragraphs, and you know they link together well, and you know that all the facts are in there, and that the story is going to make people care, and that they're going to read right down to the end of it.

You know, there's one disturbing thing about your descriptions of writing, and that is it seems to come naturally. And if it comes naturally, how do you teach people?

I don't know. I tend to think you have to teach them to be aware of the rhythm of words, and how cleanly you can create a sentence without a lot of clutter. I read everything I write out loud. I want my stories to come across as if I'm telling someone the story face to face.

It's things like computerized tomography scans that throw a little monkey wrench in there.

Let me touch on your interpretation of events. You're writing about J.J. "He was doing well in February when Carole agreed to care for Rachel, to rock the baby until she died.

"Then one night last March, J.J. died in his crib.

"The baby who had been given a new lease on life was dead. The baby that was supposed to die, Rachel, was still alive."

You did a little interpreting there. How often can a writer do that and get away with it? How effective is it?

I don't know if I have an answer for that. You just have to know the person and make sure that the assumption you're making is correct, and that the person indeed felt that way.

That produced a strong ending for the first story.

I like to make a nice intro, so people will kind of slide into the story, and then at the end, I try to give them a fact that I've held back, or something important in the story, that will reward them for making it through to the end.

And I see this as kind of a chapter, in some ways. This first chapter is ending here and you want to know more about it. So you're going to try to find the next chapter.

The next story gets into the problem of treatment for Rachel: "Medical staffers inserted the feeding tube, which drips baby formula from an IV unit, but not without much discussion, Carole says. How far can they, or should they, go to keep this baby alive?" Why did you decide to mute the issue of efforts to keep Rachel alive?

One of my writing friends pointed out that that should be a bigger issue: that this child was considered a "no code." In a medical emergency you just let her die. I agree that this should have been a bigger issue, but there was really not a lot I could do, because the doctors wouldn't talk.

In another section you write about the restaurant, and a customer complaining about having the baby in the restaurant. How do you make decisions on what to keep, which incidents to include, and what to leave out?

As I came to that part of the story about how people react so differently to the baby, I just needed one precise example. This happened at a real bad time for Carole. After being at the hospital all day, and dealing with all of these kids at once, and sitting in a little fast-food restaurant and having somebody approach her like that, it completely upset her.

And the driving force for your using this incident was that you had a point you wanted to make, and this incident showed it?

Yes.

The third part is written in diary style. What are the advantages and the disadvantages for the reader?

It is natural for this particular part of the section. This is just to show life. This is just a little slice of life. You can kind of walk into their home and be with them.

The rest of the story had been presenting a lot of facts and situations and introductions. I wanted one part of the story to show life as it was, and that's why I went over and spent all this time with them.

The advantage of it is that readers feel at home. They see parts of themselves there. The fact that these people are dealing with a dying baby, but they've also got dinner to deal with, and they've got dishes, and they've got kids that need to be bathed and fed and put to bed, and there's life going on all around this baby, all around her crib in the living room.

In terms of the disadvantage, if somehow the story hadn't progressed and the discussion gotten deeper and deeper into the evening, it wouldn't have been as interesting. If the discussions about death, and how Carole felt about it, and God, if she'd said those things early in the evening, like around 6:00 or 7:00, I don't know how I would have carried the story 'til the end.

But, as it was, the longer we sat there, the deeper the discussion got, and the better the story was.

By 2 a.m. Carole is wrestling with thoughts of Rachel's death: " 'I've finally got it through my head that we're not going to save her. I finally understand and accept that.' " What happens there in terms of reader abuse?

Well, once again, it's a reality that people don't want to deal with. It's an invitation to say, "I don't really want to deal with this issue, and I'm going to shut the section here, and I'm going to lay it down, and I'm not going to continue it."

Nobody wants to deal with a dying baby, but the story here is that somebody has to. I mean, you couldn't just leave this baby in an institution some-where to die. And in this case, it's not even the bio-logical mother, it's somebody who volunteered for it, and if Carole's going to volunteer to deal with this baby on a day-to-day basis, then I think people may have some kind of obligation to read about it, and to deal with it themselves, on their own levels.

Later in the story you wrote: "Carole shakes her head. She believes Rachel has her own purpose. It could be just to tell her story, to show people—in a painful, but powerful, way—what happens when pregnant women take drugs.

"Or it could be to prepare Carole for the chil-dren yet to come. If the experts are right, if Amer-ica sinks deeper and deeper into its drug problem, there will be many more Rachels for the Caroles of the world."

It strikes me that this is part three of a series, and in some sense, that's the "nut graph."

Yes.

You didn't have a strong temptation to put that near the beginning, say in the fourth paragraph?

No. It naturally fell there. The whole helpless feel-ing came out in that discussion. This was as good a place as any to put that information.

There are lighter moments. Early in the fourth story you wrote: "Nancy Gish knocks on the front door, but no one hears it. She comes in any-way, as she has so many times before, carrying a country doctor's black bag with a city doctor's beeper attached to it." A nice play on words. There's no humor, really, but that's one of those moments away from the sadness of the story.

Yes. I do a lot of observation. There are a lot of times when someone will be talking, and I realize that what they're saying is not necessarily going to make it into the story. It may have already been said or whatever, and I'll do a lot of notes on what color people's eyes are, and how they sit in the chair, and the things that they're wearing, and the things that they're carrying, and the way their hands move as they're talking.

You've talked about rewards. That's a different type of reward for the reader, the reward of seeing things through colorful language.

There's another interesting passage in which you interpret Carole's feelings: "You can only balance on an ethical tightrope so long. After a while, you either fall or jump."

She was in an incredible situation, because she had decided to make the funeral arrangements, yet she had the baby's pediatrician telling her that he didn't think it was necessary. She and I had incredibly long phone calls in that week as she tried to deal with this, about whether to go ahead or not.

At some point, I became a person for her to confide in, because she knew I'd listen. A lot of people didn't understand why she was doing what she was doing, and so she made a lot of calls to me to tell me what was going on, but then they would result in these long, long discussions in which she would tell me basically how she felt, right down to the nitty-gritty.

I want you to talk about ethics. Tell me about the fairness of the story. Is this fair to the Whites?

I think that they were willing participants in it. They opened their lives to me from the beginning. They were under a lot of scrutiny. I sat there with a magnifying glass on this family for four months, but they were very willing to go with it, and had decided that if I had wanted to be there at the death, that I could be.

Is that the determining factor, then, whether they were willing or not?

Yes, I think it was.

I asked you earlier, but was it fair to Rachel's mother?

Boy, that's a tough one. People have wanted me to try to track down Rachel's mother to see what happened with the baby that was born a year later, and I have some ethical problems with that. As my husband said, "Look what you did to her life. Why bother her any more?"

And that holds me back. Once the section came out, I'm sure she saw it, and I'd invaded part of her life that she...she certainly didn't ask for. But in some ways, by having the baby under the circumstances that she did, it made it fair game.

Was it fair to you? Is it fair to you to spend that much time, that close?

It's something I had wanted to do for a long, long time, to see what would happen if I did it. I needed to throw myself into something.

Believe me, there were discussions at home when I said, "Look. I'm going to put heart and soul into this, and I'm going to be writing between midnight and 4 a.m. sometimes, and I'm going to be distracted, and I may not be the best mother and wife for the next four months." But in discussing it with my husband and my daughter, who is 8, we decided that this story was very important to tell. It was a hard thing for me to do. Having two children of my own, it was...I lost a baby in the process as well. So it was a hard one to do, but I felt really good about the outcome.

You say you lost a baby in the process. You're talking about Rachel?

Yes.

Tell me about covering Rachel's death.

Well, we thought we would want to be present. In the very beginning, I began leaving numbers of where I might be able to be reached over the weekend in case she took this dramatic turn for the worse, because we thought that we would want to be there and watch this all happen. And the amazing part is, by the end, I could have been present at the death. They called me about 3:00 and the baby died about 5:00. They called me and I said that, at this point, I thought that it was a very private time for Carole and her family, and I was not going to subject them to photographs or me taking notes in the corner. I had said my goodbyes the day before to this baby, and at this point, I would let them grieve alone.

That was a real hard decision to make in some ways, but at the same time, I knew I had everything I needed for the story, that the important thing was that she had lived, not that she died.

In October, we set November 12 as our publishing date. And so we worked toward that, and she just kept going a little more downhill, a little more downhill, and then she died on November 8, four days before the section came out. The section was put out in the Sunday paper on the 12th, and her funeral was the next morning.

I don't see that as a coincidence, in some ways. I'm not an incredibly spiritual person, but I tend to think that her message was given and that there was no reason to hang around anymore. And so, when she died that close to the publishing date, I was not surprised. I know that's probably going to sound funny.

No. That sounds real.

I did not wait until Rachel died to begin writing her story. I was afraid that at that point I would be so saddened, or in an aggrieved state myself, that somehow the same feelings from the initial notes that I'd taken wouldn't come across. And so I began writing the first three parts of Rachel's story before she had taken that very serious turn for the worse. When we knew that she was definitely going downhill, I immediately went home and began writing the first three parts, so it would seem as upbeat as it was.

What about after the story? I have an interest in what happens to reporters after difficult stories, and I don't know of any more difficult than this. What happened to you in late November?

I took two weeks off after the section. I just felt like I needed it for kind of a buffer zone, a transition time, for me to get back into writing fitness columns, fashion pages, and things like that again. I basically stayed home and spent time with my family.

It was kind of awkward trying to reintegrate myself into the staff, after taking four months to do one story, one section. It was very hard to come back and have someone say, "You have a food story due for next Tuesday and you've got the next two days to do it in."

I think I rebelled, in some ways. I mean, I know what it's like now to spend time on a project, and really put heart and soul into it. The rest of my writing seemed very superficial and very trivial to me for a while. Now, I'm trying to readjust to life again, but I'll say I am looking for the next project.

I don't want to end without mentioning the ending of your story: "Rachel's mother, who declined to be interviewed for this special report, is due to have another baby in December."

How did you get that information, and why did you decide to use it as the kicker?

Carole had told me from the beginning that Rachel's mother was pregnant again, but I needed a verification of that. I mentioned that fact to various people who would know and watched them nod their heads. I'd say, "Oh, I hear she's pregnant again," and have people look at me and nod their heads. I knew that that would be the ending of the story from the very, very beginning. Because the story goes on and on.

David Von Drehle
Deadline Writing

DAVID VON DREHLE grew up in Aurora, Colorado, and graduated from the University of Denver, where he double-majored in English and philosophy. He edited his college paper and worked nights and weekends for *The Denver Post* as a sports writer, the sum total of his journalism education. On a Marshall Scholarship, he attended Oxford University for two years, receiving a master's degree. He joined *The Miami Herald* in 1985, and a year later became a city desk general assignment reporter, covering the campaign for casino gambling, the Florida legislative session that established the lottery, and the Pope's visit to the United States. Von Drehle has just become chief of *The Miami Herald*'s one-man bureau in New York City, where he bosses himself around.

Shaken survivors witness pure fury

SEPTEMBER 23, 1989

CHARLESTON, S.C.—It's noon on Thursday at Folly Beach, a stretch of sand raised a few inches above the surrounding tidal marsh and sprinkled with undistinguished bungalows and weathered seafood shacks.

It's gray, lightly sprinkling. Not unusual for a September afternoon. But big breakers are sending foam over the sea wall and the houses are deserted. The town has the eerie feeling of an unnaturally empty place—like a dusty street in a dime Western just before the bad guys arrive.

Hurricane Hugo is 12 hours away.

Tension grows through the afternoon. Every little gust of air, every spit of rain, every new shade of gray cloud is searched for meaning. With each new breeze, people speed their pace, tighten their jaws.

The streets empty. Traffic jams the roads out of town. Forecasters said gale-force winds might arrive by 3 p.m., but at 5, the palms and elms and oaks are still swaying gently.

At 5:30, as journalists and other thrill-seekers tour the Battery in a gentle rain, visibility drops suddenly. The famous sights from the harbor's edge—like Fort Moultrie, of Revolutionary War fame, and Fort Sumter, where the Civil War began—vanish in the fog.

Then rain comes, warm and straight and thick. The gale arrives next, driving the warm rain ahead of it. A statue honoring the Confederate war dead, a bronze nude brandishing a broadsword, confronts the storm wearing nothing but a fig leaf.

False alarm. The wind and rain die down. But they will be back.

From the television comes the news that Hugo is gaining speed and fury. This will be one of the rare Category 4 storms to hit the United States. Hugo is six hours away.

Sundown, and gray drains from the sky, leaving only black. The tension rises another notch. In the gloaming, the trees ball and buck in the rising winds.

By 9 p.m., the gale is gusting so hard you have to lean into it to make headway, like a street mime.

OUTAGES BLACK OUT AREA

Miami Herald photographer Jon Kral and I hope to make it to hotel rooms near the Charleston airport, 10 miles inland. As we leave downtown, a main power station gives out, and the streets become darker, more menacing.

Water swirls and snakes across the highway as we drive. The rain falls almost horizontally. Broken branches and loose garbage skid over the pavement, and the gusts are now high enough to rock the car as it creeps across Charleston's high bridges.

It's dark in all directions—power failures spread black like it was paint. The failures come quickly and rhythmically, almost as if someone were flipping a row of switches.

The manmade glow is replaced by startling eruptions of muffled light—huge lightning storms showing through the furious shroud.

A rock-and-roll station pledges to stay with us through the hurricane. "Your Hurricane Hugo station!" the DJ cries. Then he announces that the eye of the storm is just two hours away, headed straight for us— "so whatever you do, don't drive!"

Within a few minutes, the station is off the air. The storm becomes too much.

WINDS SHIFT INTO OVERDRIVE

The hotel turns out to be unprepared, but Kral produces a roll of duct tape from his bag and we strip asterisks onto each pane. At 10:30, the room lights go brown, then die, struggle back, then fail for good.

Outside, the air is screaming at the same pitch that wind reaches through a cracked window on an interstate highway. The howl is strangely pleasant, because we make the mistake of thinking that this is about as bad as it will get.

The noise halts briefly, just for a second or two, then comes back at a much higher, much more urgent pitch. After five minutes of that, Hugo clutches and shifts again to an even higher level. The winds step up like a sports car going through the gears—except that Hugo has many more gears.

With each new step, the barometric pressure drops, and we can feel the changes in our ears. At 11:30, we dress to go out into the storm, but quickly change our minds when Hugo jumps three gears in five minutes.

From somewhere inside the shrieking noise come the muffled reports of snapping trees, popping windshields, and sand hitting the windows like pellets.

Water in the toilet bowl rocks and swirls as Hugo howls through the city's sewers. Wind gusts from the light fixtures. The panes pull at their window frames.

A SOUND OF PURE FURY

Frightened families leave their rooms and walk nervously down darkened stairwells to the leaking lobby. At the bottom of one stairwell, we watch as the sucking wind tries to wrench open a double-bolted fire door.

First the air yanks, then slips its fingers into the tiny gap between door and door frame, then strains at the heavy steel structure until the door actually *bends*.

Then the awful clutching silence, and the wind returns, up another impossible gear.

By midnight, as the worst of the fury roars nightmarishly over Charleston, the very walls tremble and quake.

The noise of a killer hurricane has been compared to a passing freight train so many times it has become a sort of journalists' joke. "Let me guess —did it sound like a train?"

But to me, this doesn't sound like a train. It sounds like the harsh intake of a dentist's suction tube, greatly amplified and always increasing. Or the roar of a seashell a billion times over. Or Niagara, if only Niagara cranked up its volume each time your ears got adjusted to it.

Most of all, it sounds like pure fury.

One of Kral's taped windows explodes minutes after we leave the room. When we come back, it's impossible to open the door, the wind is so strong. We have to wait for a pause between gears, then drive with our shoulders.

A TEMPEST IN A MOTEL ROOM

Thick rain is blowing horizontally through the room. Thanks to the duct tape, the shattered glass is in a neat pile on the floor. We shout over the gale.

In the bathroom, the swirling winds have pulled the Sheetrock ceiling away from the walls. For the rest of the tempest, Hugo works on tearing the room apart. Gusts of 25 miles per hour come through the ceiling. The nails and screws groan at the strain.

The winds are much wilder, much more intense than anything I have experienced before. The difference between 100-mph winds and 130-mph winds is so great that they ought to have different names.

At five minutes past midnight, the noise begins gearing down rapidly. By 12:15, it's almost still. Some of us venture outside and inspect the damage by flashlight.

A thick steel flagpole, barely anything to it to resist the wind, is bent at a 60-degree angle. An ancient Pontiac, finned and weighty, has been shoved several feet into a Saab. A Chrysler New Yorker is deposited on the sidewalk.

Along the windward side of the hotel, the windows of the cars are consistently shattered, as if by methodical vandals. "I'll sell this new Honda right now for $9,000," says a distraught owner.

Then he sees his girlfriend's matching car with matching wounds. "Two for $18,000," he says.

COMPLETE STILLNESS

The ground is thick with tree limbs and glass and aluminum and shingles and bits of plastic signs. Bits of Sheraton, bits of McDonald's.

At 12:30, complete stillness. We're in the middle of Hugo's eye. It's still and silent and hot and humid on a landscape covered with debris. It feels like surfacing from a bomb shelter at the end of the world.

"I thought you were supposed to see stars when you're in the eye," someone says.

We all look up. No stars. Then we notice a highway sign, still attached to its pole, jutting up near an old Impala. The sign, we realize, must have been uprooted a quarter-mile away.

It has been driven, like a javelin, through the side of the car, and stuck there as firmly as Excalibur in the stone.

Five minutes pass. Then comes a tiny puff of breeze, so faint as to be imperceptible—except that we are waiting for it so intently. Within a few seconds, a faint drizzle follows. Half a minute after that, the breeze and drizzle are rattling shredded metal like spook-house ghosts.

Then, just before the wind resumes lifting and twirling debris, Orion's belt and a few stars peep through, low in the northern sky. Then disappear.

WIND BLOWS IN OPPOSITE WAY

Back inside, water pours through the lobby ceiling and sloshes on the floor. Now the wind blows the opposite way, drawing the curtains out through Kral's gaping window. They snapped so hard against the adjacent panes we fear they will break, so we rip the curtains from the rods.

By 12:45 Hugo is back near peak fury. Kral points a light into the storm to illuminate the movements of the rain. It zings through the air, up, sideways, diagonally, sometimes downward. It whips and swirls, a true maelstrom.

Now a new row of cars catches the full fury, and new stands of trees. Windshields explode and trees crack like firecrackers. The noise is swallowed in the roar of the storm.

Again, the ears are popping, as the barometric pressure returns. In this respect, Hugo is a lot like flying on a jet—on the *outside*.

The backside of the storm seems to gear up and fade more quickly than the leading edge, but in fact it does not. Time is speeding up. The storm pumped so much adrenaline, and sharpened the senses so acutely, that time slowed, and now it is resuming its normal pace.

The winds drop as Hugo recedes. Almost immediately, it is hard to recall how fiercely it blew. And almost impossible to believe.

Observations and questions

1) David Von Drehle begins this story with a time marker: "It's noon on Thursday at Folly Beach..." Find all the time markers in this story and study how Von Drehle uses them as transitions and guideposts for the reader.

2) This piece begins in the present tense ("It's noon..."), whereas readers expect the traditional past tense. Readers would also expect a shift out of the present tense rather soon, since writers seldom stay in it long. Think about the hazards of frustrating such reader expectations, and the opportunities.

3) Writers generally avoid the present tense because of the difficulties of sustaining it. Study Von Drehle's whole piece to find places where the present tense may have caused awkwardness.

4) This story works because, among other things, Von Drehle constantly raises the level of tension for the reader. Study how he manipulates his readers' emotions, and reflect on how you might use his techniques in daily newswriting. And don't say your editor wouldn't let you.

5) Von Drehle unifies his story with imagery of cars and driving. Find all these images and study how he weaves them in. Do the same with images of darkness, gears, and notches. How does he keep so many repeated images from becoming tiresome?

6) Von Drehle first uses the first person in paragraph 12: "*Miami Herald* photographer Jon Kral and I..." Why do reporters avoid the first person? Do you find Von Drehle's first-person narration effective? Why?

7) News writers generally avoid using lots of adjectives and adverbs. Why? Find all the adjectives and adverbs in this piece, and see how many you can cut without hurting their scenes.

8) Von Drehle highlights a cliche as he gives it new life: "The noise of a killer hurricane has been compared to a passing freight train so many times it has become a sort of journalists' joke. 'Let me guess—did it sound like a train?'" How can you use cliches without becoming trite? How can you see beyond cliches during your reporting so you transcend them when you write?

9) Von Drehle pictures the storm as an unseen malevolent being, attacking people, as in this sentence: "The failures come quickly and rhythmically, almost as if someone were flipping a row of switches." Find the other instances of such personification, and think about how you might use this device to represent forces.

10) Find all the trade names in this story. Why do reporters generally leave them out, or make them generic ("Rolex" becomes "wristwatch")? Would this story improve if we smudged the brand names? Why?

11) Von Drehle says he worked hard on the comparisons in this piece. Such analogies help the reader understand the unknown by comparing it to the known. But consider this one: "It feels like surfacing from a bomb shelter at the end of the world." Why would Von Drehle compare something no one has ever experienced to convey something he has experienced himself? Why not just tell us?

12) Divide this story into parts. Notice how Von Drehle devotes a smaller proportion of his space to the second half of the hurricane. Would it improve the story to flesh out the last part?

13) Study Von Drehle's kicker: "The winds drop as Hugo recedes. Almost immediately, it is hard to recall how fiercely it blew. And almost impossible to believe." Would the ending improve if we deleted the last sentence? How else could Von Drehle have ended this story?

14) Now that you've experienced a hurricane through Von Drehle's story, are you more eager or less eager to cover one from inside the eye yourself?

A conversation with
David Von Drehle

DON FRY: Who taught you to write, David?

DAVID VON DREHLE: I learned a lot about writing from one of my college teachers at the University of Denver. Frank Seeburger was just a classic spacey, off-the-wall, stereotypical Hollywood-type philosophy professor. We spent an entire summer writing one paragraph.

One paragraph? [Laughter]

Yeah, he gave us a two- or three-page reading from Wittgenstein, and our job was to write one paragraph saying what Wittgenstein was trying to say in his three pages. He'd go through our papers and attack them at the most fundamental levels of conception and construction. And he might write three pages of critique of one paragraph, and then give it back to you, and tell you to write it again for next week. And right at the tail end of the summer, I was the only one in that class who got to move on to the next paragraph. [Laughter]

I see. What did that teach you about writing?

It seems like a simple concept, but it certainly took me a long time to learn it: You can't write clearly about something that you're not thinking clearly about. I always had a minor gift for turn of phrase and embellishment, which had carried me a long way, as it can carry a lot of writers a long way.

Indeed.

And Frank didn't care about the embellishments or the flourishes or anything else. He wanted to see if the thing was a clear statement of a clearly understood idea. And until it was, he wasn't going to be happy with it. At the end of the whole exercise, I was sold on the concept that there was a connection between thinking and writing.

Who else helped your writing?

Gene Miller, our two-time Pulitzer Prize winner at the *Herald,* who is now the newspaper's writing coach, has taught a lot of journalists a lot about reporting....

Certainly a model of clarity himself.

Exactly, and I learned from Gene another of these simple ideas, that if had I taken journalism courses I might have learned in the second week, but I was sort of slow learning. I learned from Gene that there's no substitute for detail, and no amount of pretty flourishes will bring points home or bring your copy to life quite the way the telling detail will.

That certainly shows in your hurricane story.

Thanks. I had to keep reminding myself all the way through: "Now pay attention. Watch what the hell's going on." [Laughter]

What were you doing before you got the hurricane assignment?

I did an investigation of a couple of guys on death row who appeared to be innocent. I got to spend about a month tromping around through trailer courts and digging through old murder files in rural Florida and Georgia, and wound up doing a three-part series on that case. That got me interested in the death penalty. So I spent a portion of the first half of '88 working on the death penalty from a public policy point of view, in terms of its cost and its efficiency, an analysis separate from the moral or emotional arguments. I covered Ted Bundy's execution. Then the *Herald* decided to start covering the environment in Florida and nationally in a more aggressive fashion, and they asked me to take that beat for a year.

You've skipped all the traditional training grounds, like night cops and courts and schools.

Well, I've had to pick it up in small fits and starts. Just this past fall, we had a big trial down in Miami of this Hispanic police officer who shot a couple of black guys on a motorcycle and set off a riot. We put a full court press on it, and I was added to our regular courts reporter, and the two of us team-covered it. By the end of three months, I had some sense of knowing my way around the courthouse. And the same with cops, getting thrown into stories, and having to flounder around and try to pick it up real fast.

But you didn't go through the grueling night cops experience of having to get everything right on very little information.

That's exactly right.

Tell me about the hurricane, which happened in September 1989, right?

Yeah. In Florida, when a big hurricane comes up, everyone's thrown into the breach. The *Herald* has a tradition of having two or three people on the staff at any given time who, in addition to their ordinary duties, get assigned to anchor big breaking stories, such as natural disasters and huge cop stories. We call them "anchors."

Some papers call them "parachuters."

Right. So I had evolved into an anchor. A year before, Hurricane Gilbert, the most powerful hurricane on record, had roared across the Caribbean. I had begged through the entire thing to get sent somewhere to get out and muck around and find some bad weather. And they told me that I couldn't go because they needed me to sit in the office and take dispatches from all the heroic reporters who were out there in the middle of things, and piece them together into stories. Call up the Weather Bureau, and that kind of thing.

So they owed you one.

Yeah. It was my turn to go out.

How far ahead were you sent up to Charleston?

The hurricane blew in Thursday, September 21, so I got there about 10:30 p.m. on Wednesday the 20th.

What do you do first when a hurricane's supposed to show up?

That was exactly the question I asked myself. I rented a great big, heavy car, thinking I might go more places after the thing was over. Then I drove into town and looked for a grocery store, because we were still within about 30 minutes of our dead line for Thursday's paper. I interviewed people who were clearing supplies off the shelves, getting ready for the thing to hit, and went out to the pay phone and fed that for our last edition. And I bought some bottled water and some crackers because somebody had been decent enough to tell me that I should do that. Coming from Denver, I would never have thought to make any preparations myself; I would have wandered out the morning after it hit, looking for a place to have breakfast. [Laughter] Then I did what all print reporters do these days: I went to the hotel and turned on CNN.

Right.

Then I got a little sleep. Thursday morning, my photographer, Jon Kral, arrived. We started driving around, trying to get out to the beachfront communities. Then we tried to find the local newspaper to figure out what they were going to do to try to keep their power on, more for Jon than for me because a photographer is so dependent on darkrooms.

By about 6:00, the weather was starting to get pretty bad. But the 6:00 forecast from the National Hurricane Center said the hurricane had taken a little wobble to the north, and that suddenly made everyone in Miami think that Jon and I should move further north up the coast to Myrtle Beach, which was about an hour's drive.

Were you calling in to the desk?

Yeah. You really feel out on a limb, so I tend to call in every couple of hours. With CNN and the wires and the Weather Channel, the desk has voluminous amounts of information. So I call in not so much to give them information as to find out what they know that I don't know.

Then what happened?

We had a long discussion about whether we should pull out of Charleston and go to Myrtle Beach. I was fortunate to have Jon around, who's been through a number of hurricanes; this was my first hurricane. There's a rule around the *Herald* that we always forget by the time the next big hurricane comes along: Don't chase them too much. Many times a reporter has made one last heroic effort to get to one more city down the road, and the hurricane comes crashing in wherever he or she had just left. [Laughter]

Naturally. Why did you decide to stay put in Charleston?

Well, Jon argued two things. One was that we had found a home base there; we'd scouted out Charleston. We'd be going from a known to an unknown just as a huge hurricane was blowing in, just asking for a lot of confusion. And second, Charleston is a pretty big city, and there were hundreds of thousands of people trying to get out of it. Kral wisely pointed out that the roads would be so jammed that we'd never get anywhere near anywhere. Jon carried the day, and I'm eternally grateful that he did, because otherwise I would have been out of play.

Then what happened?

Downtown Charleston is at very low elevation, and it suddenly dawned on us that if this hurricane flooded the city, we would be minus our cars. Between 8:00 and 9:00, the storm was really starting to pick up, so we decided to try to make a move to higher ground, from downtown Charleston out to the airport, which is about eight or 10 miles inland, and about 80 or 100 feet higher in elevation.

Right. Did you have a hotel reservation?

We didn't, and I didn't think we'd be able to get one. We were talking about trying to persuade somebody to let us sit in the lobby overnight. I picked up the phone and called the Sheraton, and they said, "Yeah, we've got plenty of rooms."

Everybody was out of town! [Laughter]

Yeah. Apparently, everybody went way inland, and they were smart to do that, because the worst damage was in the airport area. We would have been perfectly all right to stay downtown.

When we got there, it was a project just getting the door of the hotel open and closed again. The wind was starting to blow that hard. We went up to our rooms and settled in. I still had in mind that to describe what a hurricane was like, I needed to go outside in the middle of it....

Clearly a man who's never been out in one. [Laughter]

Clearly. So Kral was telling me I was crazy, but he's a typical photographer, completely daredevil and lunatic, so I talked him into going out there to take a look. I was familiar with the spring chinook winds coming down the eastern front of the Rockies, 90-, 100-mph winds. I'd been out in that sort of thing, and it's sort of fun in a weird way. But just in the time it took to put on our rain gear, it went from sounding like a really big windstorm, the sort of thing I was used to, to something that was just so much...just unbelievably more intense. And it was such a dramatic change that there was no question of even thinking about going outside.

Not even with a daredevil photographer!

Right. [Laughter] So there we are in this dark hotel, and this storm is getting worse and worse. Until all the radio stations went off the air at 11:00 or 11:30, we'd keep hearing these reports that this hurricane was really winding itself up, just as it made landfall, and had gone up from a Category 3 to a Category 4, and kept intensifying. This was really bad news.

Were you afraid?

I never thought that this hurricane would blow an eight-story Sheraton over! On the other hand, we were standing in a stairwell, because you always hear that stairwells are the best-constructed part of a building. And the concrete...the cinderblock walls are shaking, and the wind just keeps getting louder and louder, and more and more furious. It crossed my mind that it had better stop...stop getting worse! [Laughter]

The concrete was bending?

Right. And there was one of those super-reinforced outside emergency doors with those huge fire latches on top of it, with the big dead bolts and the heavy steel frame set into the concrete wall. And the wind was creating a vacuum that was drawing the door away from the frame, and we were getting these gusts of wind into the stairwell rushing through that tiny crack, and that hurricane really wanted to get that door opened, to the point that this solid steel door was bending around the dead bolt. There was a real prospect that the frame would tear out of the wall.

Wow! You just personified the hurricane. You said, "...that hurricane really wanted to get that door opened." Did you feel that way then?

It's almost irresistible to give the storm a personal... a malevolent quality. You do think of it as having a will and control and just this intense fury about it, wanting to tear things apart.

Right. You have a very graphic passage about this stairwell scene. Was this part written from memory?

I was taking notes.

You were standing in a stairwell, about to be killed, and you were taking notes?!

Yeah. I was jotting down little one-word things. Early in the day, I was able to take leisurely notes. Then as the evening wore on, and taking care of ourselves became more and more a central focus, the note-taking got to the point where I was just trying to write down single words that would help me remember what order things happened in, and also what it was like. So we went back to our rooms...

Wait.... Why did you leave the stairwell? You were safe there.

Well, because we wanted to know what else was going on, and what it was like in other parts of the hotel. We came out of the stairwell on the fifth floor, and there's this howling, shrieking wind that seems, in some strange way, a little worse than it was elsewhere. We had adjoining rooms, and we put the key in Jon's door and pushed, and it was as if the door were bricked up. You just couldn't move it. And we figured out that one of the windows must have blown out.

When you busted in, what was it like in there?

It was...it was unlike any other room I've ever been in. We had sheets of rain blowing horizontally through the room, and my real concern was that the glass would be blowing around in the air. But we barely went in, and crouched back in the clothes alcove, kind of a lee area from the worst of the wind. We were able to figure out that things were not flying around through the air, and we ran in. It felt like playing soldiers back as a little boy, because we were dashing around and hiding behind things and trying to stay low, because we were concerned that another window would blow out and send glass all over the place. So we pulled all of Jon Kral's cameras out of his room and moved them next door into my room, and then, as quickly as we could, left the room.

Then the hurricane's eye came over, and you went outside.

Right. The striking thing to me was how quickly the eye came in. The storm had taken so long to gather, had taken all day to get there, and then it went from this peak fury to absolute stillness in a matter of 10 or 15 minutes. The hurricane is such an assault on your senses. It is unbelievably loud and terrifying. Your nerves are so completely on edge; you're just totally keyed up. And suddenly all that's gone, and that enormous noise suddenly stops, and everything seems just intensely quiet.

Yes. I've been in the eye of a hurricane, and of course, you know what's going to happen next: The backside is coming.

Yeah, and that's kind of hard to believe while you're in it, or it was for me. I knew it was coming, but it was hard for that to register emotionally. The other thing that struck me was how warm it was. When you have bad weather where I'm from, it's usually a blizzard. So I was struck by the heat and humidity and stillness, and we just walked around in the parking lot of the hotel with our flashlights shining here and there, and people totally quiet, not talking at all, except to exclaim when they came across another piece of unbelievable damage.

But weren't you interviewing people out there?

No.

Why not? [Long pause] I'm not criticizing you; that's a question.

No. No. I'm not taking it that way. Whatever is striking about my story grew out of conversations with a couple of my editors for several years, through a number of hurricane seasons. We would sit around after a hurricane had blown through somewhere, and we would talk about how the stories had been good and complete and interesting, and all of that, but how hungry we were as readers for a story that just said what it's like to go through one. A story that didn't necessarily do anything else, didn't have body counts in it, didn't do anything by the book, *not* interviewing a number of different people, *not* describing heroic escapes. I'm not running down all those things that make great stories. We decided that if we found ourselves in the middle of a big hurricane, that the story that needed to be done, that is not typically done, that readers would want to see, is just a simple account: "Jeez. What was it like?"

So you weren't out there just sopping up random information like a sponge. You were projecting what the story would be like as you were gathering material, right?

Right. I knew what I had in mind. Given that, I made a number of decisions on how to use my time, and they wound up being counterintuitive against basic things that you learn as a journalist. I would tell myself: "No, don't go ask somebody else what they felt, or what they thought about it, which would be the natural thing for a newspaper reporter to do. Take that same amount of time and spend it focusing intently and really thinking about what's happening to you."

One of the reasons you could be counterintuitive was that you had had conversations with your editors ahead of time. One reason reporters only do the normal things is that they think if they don't do the normal things, their editors will yell at them when they get back. And they're usually right, alas. Whereas you'd had conversations about these matters with your editors.

Absolutely right. If there's a journalism lesson here, it's to sit down and talk and think with your editors about what the story's going to be. And conversely, for editors to think about what story they want ahead of time. And not the morning after it's happened; it's too late for that.

Right. Because you don't know what to look for the morning after.

That's right. You might go to your notebook and find that you have lots of great quotes from the people who were standing next to you in the stairwell, but that you were too busy talking to them to notice what it was really like.

Right. So then you went back in, because the eye was moving over you.

That's right. I remember just this little puff of breeze, something you would never even notice on an ordinary day, and all of us jerking up and looking at each other and starting to move for the door.

And then very quickly the wind picked up, and then there was this mist, and then the rain started falling. We went back up to the rooms. Jon had this wonderful flashlight that you could put around your neck, which would cast light on whatever you had in your hands, and you'd have your hands free. So I put this thing on and sat down on the floor in the room and just started writing in my notebook, fast and furious...

Were you taking notes, or were you writing the story?

At the time, I thought I was taking notes, but it turned out that I was writing the story. I wrote as fast as I could, just chronologically, everything that had happened, and everything that I'd felt....

Oh, you weren't writing what was happening at that moment. You were writing retrospectively?

Yeah, I was writing retrospectively. If the story is 40 or 42 inches, you've got about 39 or 40 inches up to the time when the eye passes, and about two sentences about what it was like after the eye passed. Because I was writing the story after the eye passed, it all seemed anticlimactic; it had already happened.

So you were writing while the storm was still raging. Wasn't that a little distracting? [Laughter]

Well, what was distracting was that the poor hotel manager kept coming by our room and pounding on the door and begging us to get out, but we had decided that if the storm hadn't blown the hotel over on the first pass, it wouldn't blow it over on the second. And I didn't want to sit in a lobby with the water 6 inches deep, having people walking over to me and asking me, "Jeez, what are you doing? Are you a reporter?"

Did the storm blow on out while you stayed in the room and wrote, or did you go out and report some more?

The storm blew out. For about two hours, I wrote everything I could remember until about 3:30 or 4:00 a.m. I passed out on the bed for about three hours and got up at dawn. We drove into town and started doing normal, real reporter reporting: sizing up the damage, interviewing people whose homes had been destroyed, that kind of story. We reported in town for about four or five hours. The power and the phones were out in town, so by late morning we decided to head up the road about 65 or 70 miles to Columbia, South Carolina, where there's a Knight-Ridder paper, *The State*, so Jon would have a darkroom. We got there in the early afternoon, and I sat down and converted the rough thing that I had written the night before into the story...

Sat down at what? Did *The State* give you a terminal?

No. I used a Radio Shack model 100 laptop.

That's my favorite computer. People keep winning this prize on the Radio Shack 100, the most primitive computer in journalism. [Laughter] The thinking wins the prize, not the gear.
How long did it take you to draft the story, after you sat down in Columbia?

I think it was two or three hours, not counting the scribbling the night before.

Let's talk about some decisions. When did you decide on chronological order?

Within five or 10 minutes of sitting down and starting to write at the newspaper.

Did you consider any other structures?

I briefly considered starting at the peak of the storm in order to get a really intense lead. And I also considered starting with the morning after the storm. I discarded that idea because I realized that morning wasn't part of the story. And as much as I would have preferred a more intense lead on this story, I didn't want to get in the way of the story. I knew I had a good story. I knew that it had been one hell of a hurricane, and that people would be interested in reading what it was like. So, given the amount of time I had and the limits of my writing skills and gifts, the best thing for me to do was just get out of the way and tell the thing.

Good call.

As a newspaper journalist, first and foremost, your function is to communicate information clearly. You need a compelling reason to do anything other than a chronological account of almost anything, because that's the natural way to tell things. So generally, I think of almost everything I do in terms of writing a lead to get people into the story, then taking them through the information step by step, and then ending it on a high note....

But...

But this story doesn't have a lead, and it doesn't end on a high note. It just has the step-by-step middle.

Well, it does have a beginning. Here's your lead or top or whatever:
     "CHARLESTON, S.C.—It's noon on Thursday at Folly Beach, a stretch of sand raised a few inches above the surrounding tidal marsh and sprinkled with undistinguished bungalows and weathered seafood shacks.
     "It's gray, lightly sprinkling. Not unusual for a September afternoon. But big breakers are sending foam over the sea wall and the houses are deserted. The town has the eerie feeling of an unnaturally empty place—like a dusty street in a dime Western just before the bad guys arrive.
     "Hurricane Hugo is 12 hours away."
Do you consider that a lead, or just the start of the middle? [Laughter]

It's a lead because of that third graph: "Hurricane Hugo is 12 hours away." The top of the story couldn't have worked without that graph, because I would have been asking people to bear with me for an awfully long time without telling them what the payoff would be. So in that sense, it's a lead. I woke up in Charleston that morning of Thursday, the 21st, and it was gray out, and it was spitting a little rain, but it was no different from any other possible September day. And it wasn't until I got out to Folly Beach at noon and saw those waves crashing in, blowing over the sea wall, that it really hit me, that there was a big storm coming. And so, in terms of my experience of the hurricane, that was where it started.

The second decision, to write in the first person, was made in the discussion with the editors earlier, right?

Right, although I hate writing in the first person.

Why?

Well, because I don't like to read stories that have a lot of "I's" in them. In general, I don't really care much about who the reporter is. I don't like reporters as celebrities. But for this story, because of the way we reported it, because of the things we talked about earlier, there was no way to write it in the third person. I started out wanting to...I probably shouldn't confess this, because I should be saying that I had planned out every inch of the story before I started.

Nah. Even *I* don't do that.

But you go down about 10 inches of a 40-inch story before you see the first "I."

Right. "*Miami Herald* photographer Jon Kral and *I* hope to make it to hotel rooms near the Charleston airport, 10 miles inland."

All the way down to that point, I was still hoping that I could do it without putting the capital "I" in the story. Then I realized I couldn't, because we had to get the consciousness of the story from place to place. There had to be somebody who was going from place to place.

Right, you're the reader's representative. You're the guy I can empathize with in the story and the scene.

Yeah. The typical disaster story would have somebody that you're quoting who had had terrible things happen to them. And that's the person the reader can latch onto and say, "Jeez, there's a guy like me, having these things happen to him." But in this story, because of the way I'd reported it, I didn't have that person. I was that person.

Right. Your third decision was to write in the present tense instead of the past. When did you decide that, and why?

I didn't. I filed this thing shifting back and forth in tenses.

You did?

Yeah, and more accidentally than deliberately. I have a terrible problem paying attention to what tense I'm in. In that sense, I write at about a third-grade level, because I just lose track of it. This story ran pretty much word for word as I filed it, but my editors did a yeoman's job in getting it all in the correct tense. All but one place.

So the editors converted it to the present tense?

Yeah, we talked about it, and we decided that there was a more urgent sound to the present tense.

Right. But they conferred with you? They didn't just do it?

Yeah, we conferred, but it was after the story was filed that we finally made the decision on present tense. And when you write a story, other people see its virtues, and all you can see when you read it again are the things you wish you'd done different-ly. And if you look six graphs from the end, you see: "They *snapped* so hard against the adjacent panes we *fear* they *will break*, so we *rip* the curtains from the rods." That's an artifact of the original sto-ry, the one uncaught tense problem. In fact, that whole sentence is a disaster. It's not clear whether I'm talking about the curtains or the panes.

Well, I'm going to leave it alone when I edit the book.

I was afraid you were going to say that. [Laughter] I wish I could say, "Yes, I made a clear and cogent decision to put it in the present tense and did it," but I made a mishmash of the tenses.

Well, you've got to leave some things like that alone so your reader knows it's handmade. [Laughter]
I'm struck by the number of comparisons you use. Is that because very few people have had the experience of a hurricane, so you have to compare it to things?

There were two reasons. That's the first one. I kept thinking of myself 24 hours before, having not grown up in the South. Certainly in our readership area, we've got a lot of people who didn't grow up in the South. And never having seen or heard any-thing like it, I wanted to have really vivid analo-gies. It's just not enough to say, "The forceful hur-ricane raked the city," because if you've been through one, that's all you have to say, and people will know what that means. But for the zillion peo-ple who haven't, that's meaningless.

Right.

The other reason, more from a personal standpoint, from a writer's standpoint, is that I've always felt that analogies were a weak spot in my writing. So in terms of self-development, I looked on this story as a chance to try to work on that...

Now wait a minute! Are you telling me that you were experimenting with style in the middle of a hurricane?

Yeah. Yeah. I was. I said, "Now, here's a chance..."

[Laughs]

Analogies don't just pop into my head, as they do for some good writers I know, and I've always been very envious of them, the way analogies just keep coming and coming and coming to them. And the only time I ever get an analogy at all is if I concentrate intently on what is happening, and laboriously go through the catalog of my other experiences to find something it matches. And so it occurred to me that this would be the opportunity to try that out.

Amazing. Let's look at some of your analogies:
   "Outside, the air is screaming *at the same pitch* that wind reaches through a cracked window on an interstate highway. The howl is strangely pleasant, because we make the mistake of thinking that this is about as bad as it will get.
   "The noise halts briefly, just for a second or two, then comes back at a much higher, much more urgent pitch. After five minutes of that, Hugo clutches and shifts again to an even higher level. The winds step up *like a sports car* going through the gears—except that Hugo has many more gears."
   How did you come up with all this car imagery?

We were sitting there in the hotel room when the storm stepped up and got a lot worse. I'm trying to pay attention to the sound of the storm, and I'm digging around for an analogy, extremely frustrated because I can't come up with anything better than the old reliable that I make fun of in the story: the passing freight train. And I had sworn to myself that I would never compare a hurricane to a passing freight train, in the same way when I was a sports writer, I'd sworn that I'd never never quote a coach saying that his team had given 110 percent. [Laughter] And then down in the stairwell and out into the eye, I'm wracking my brain, and nothing is coming to me. And then I was pouring out the notes in this stream-of-consciousness scribbling, as the backside of the storm was blowing over, and I don't know how it happened, but it just suddenly popped into my mind that it was exactly the sound that we used to make as kids when we were pretending to be cars. And it suddenly popped into my brain when I stopped thinking about it.

Of course, and that led to the gear image.

Right.

It's a wonderful image, because everybody can remember that one, and it keeps coming and coming and coming.

I think it's the best thing in the story. And I guess I can give myself credit for thinking about it real hard, but it was serendipity that I found it.

Serendipity happens to prepared minds, as they say. [Laughter] Are you usually this literary? Let me give you an example: "It's dark in all directions—power failures spread black like it was paint."

I hate to keep giving long answers to short questions, but...in trying to develop myself as a writer, to a large extent self-taught, first I put myself through a number of years where I wrote incredibly short sentences: no dependent clauses, no adjectives, no nothing, just as spare as I could get it, sort of the Gene Miller approach. At no time did I want that to be my finished style, but I realized that I needed to get control of my writing. You've got to be able to write a simple, declarative sentence before you can write a sentence with a dependent clause in it.

Right. If every journalist practiced that, writing coaches could go out of business.

Well, it took me a long time to realize it. In the past year or so, I've been trying to add color, description, and structural complication to stories. So if you looked at what I've done over four and a half years at the *Herald,* you wouldn't find a lot of sentences like that one. But if you look at what I've done in the past year only, you would find a lot more.

So this story isn't such a watershed as one might think, in terms of your style?

Yeah. A couple of the stories I did on the environment beat in the few months before this story were a watershed. I would give myself a paragraph or two describing, for example, the Rookery Bay area between Naples and Marco Island, trying to do it with some analogies and similes and flourishes. If I screwed it up, all I'd have to do is delete those paragraphs and have the rest of the story alive. In this story, the whole piece is like that.

Is this the style you intend to use for a while?

Well, it definitely built my confidence. I was able to write this story in a very descriptive style because there was so much to describe. But you have to control yourself, and not push your material past where it will go.

So you've reached a new plateau of style, coming out of the opportunity to be on the scene during the event.

No question. And yet, unfortunately, so many reporters can get scared out of that opportunity. At
some journalism schools, teaching students to be
objective and dispassionate and those other very
valuable qualities can have the effect of scaring
them out of admitting that they were actually present somewhere.

**Right. I make my living undoing what the jour-
nalism schools teach. [Laughter]**

There are just a lot of young journalists who, if they
had been through this hurricane, would feel their
mandate was to turn to the person next to them and
ask, "What happened?"

[Laughter] Or, "How do you feel?"

Well, you're the trained observer. You're the person who went to journalism school and is paid to
pay attention, so there's an awfully good chance
that you know as well or better than the person that
you turned to what it felt like.

**Right. Did you put anything in the notebook
that you *didn't* use in the story, that you really
wished you had?**

I never went back and looked. That's a great question though. I bet if I went back and looked, there'd
be something.

**I ask that question because I teach reporters
how to throw out wonderful things that don't
help them make their point.**

You have to. If you're throwing out great stuff, that
means you've got really great stuff in a story.

Right. It's hard to learn that kind of discipline.

Oh, jeez, that's hard. Gene Miller is a great teacher
of that. You'll go word for word through a story

with him, and he'll come to something and say, "God, that's great. Gotta go." [Laughter] And you'll say, "No. No. No. That's so great." He says, "Yep. You're going to miss that for the rest of your life. You're going to read this story and hate that it's not in there. But it's gotta go." And he's always right.

Putting aside the fact that you won the prize, are you pleased with the way this story came out?

Except for that one sentence with the wrong tense. When I read the story now, it's not as compelling to me as I wish it was, but it did do what I set out to do: to tell people who'd never been in a hurricane what a hurricane is like.

Would you do it over again? Are you ready to plunge into the eye of another hurricane?

I'm not in any hurry to. But I would say that if you want to do really compelling stories about hurricanes, you should get yourself in the middle of the most destructive one in American history!

[Laughter] Right. Just order up a Category 4. Actually, for odd people like us, the hurricane isn't the adventure. Writing about it is the adventure.

Oh, yeah. And one of the adventures is the tremendous logistic problem of covering a disaster, because you lose all the luxuries you're accustomed to, that help you write a good story: the comfort of working telephones and lights and air conditioning, and television sets backing you up, and a dry bed to sleep on. There's the excitement of an endurance test to it, as well as just trying to get the words in the right order.

It gets you down to basics, the tools that always stay with you: the words.

That's right.

Diana Griego Erwin
Commentary

DIANA GRIEGO ERWIN grew up in Rosemead, a suburb of Los Angeles. She majored first in communications and then in liberal studies at California State University—Fullerton, finishing in 1984. One month after she started at *The Denver Post*, she began a series dispelling the myth that thousands of children were being abducted by strangers every year in the United States; the *Post* won the Pulitzer Prize for public service for this series. She joined *The Orange County Register* in 1988 as a features writer, becoming a columnist six months later. Her second column appears among her winning pieces here. Erwin is the first Hispanic winner of the ASNE Distinguished Writing Award.

His dreams belong to the next generation

MAY 25, 1989

His brow furrowed and the crow's-feet deepened as he struggled to understand. There was little doubt. He was confused.

The busy information clerk at the Department of Motor Vehicles in Santa Ana didn't notice.

"You need to go over there," she said, pointing across the room to the sea of people waiting. "I already told you."

It was 11 a.m. Her patience was shot for the morning.

The man pulled at the waistband of his beige work pants and scratched his sun-aged face. He stared at her, stalling for time as he tried to understand, but afraid to say he didn't.

He left, returned. The next clerk didn't speak Spanish either.

"Why can't they learn English?" she grumbled to me, the next in line.

"He probably won't," I said. "But maybe his kids will."

I had to say it. My father had been one of those kids. The ones who learn English although their parents speak Spanish at home. Schools back then didn't offer special programs; some people have told me that nuns rapped their knuckles with a ruler if they spoke Spanish—even on the playground. They learned English quickly and well that way.

But the information clerks didn't know all this, so they couldn't understand the man with the sun-aged face like I did.

I watched as he leaned against a wall where about 15 men waited. Many wore work pants and that same face, deeply lined from too much sun and too many worries.

I asked Luis Manuel Delgado why he waited.

"The lady who speaks Spanish has gone to lunch," he said.

There was no irritation in his voice, no anger at the time wasted. It was simply a fact.

I pointed out that the clerks hadn't treated him very nicely. Didn't that anger him? I wondered.

"I should know how to speak English," he said with a quiet simplicity. "This is the United States."

Delgado, 46, said he works long hours and doesn't leave in time to attend adult English classes.

He came to the United States in 1973 because two brothers and three uncles had migrated here and found better lives than the ones they left in Mexico.

Delgado worked as a bricklayer and saved enough money so his wife and two children could join him after 2-1/2 years. An uncle paid for the other two children to come.

A lifetime renter and a nobody by social standards, Delgado has big dreams for his children. He hopes they are respected by their peers and become property owners. In his old age, maybe he will live comfortably in a house owned by one of his children.

Meanwhile, he works hard and long to educate his kids. They are his future. "I am here for my children," he said proudly.

I was right about Luis Manuel Delgado.

"My kids are very good," he said. "They get good marks in school. They speak English. No accent. One wants to be a doctor.

"When they first came here I told them to study English and learn it well. Don't let them treat you like a donkey like they treat your papa."

I asked him if it didn't hurt, being treated *como un burro*, like he said.

"No, I am not a donkey and my children know it. They know I do all this for them. They are proud of me. Nothing anyone else says or does can make me sad when they have pride in me.

"And they will never be donkeys."

He nodded toward the stressed-out information clerks busily shuffling papers behind the government-issued desk. "And they won't work here," he said. "This is donkey work."

Observations and questions

1) This piece has no lead. Should columns have leads? Leads hook the reader, tell what the piece is about, and teach the reader what to expect. If a column lacks a lead, what accomplishes those tasks?

2) Diana Erwin holds the language problem until the sixth paragraph because she doesn't want to turn off readers tired of hearing about the difficulties of Spanish speakers. Does that delay serve the needs of readers who are not so put off? Rewrite the top to introduce the problem earlier, and compare your version with hers.

3) Notice the effect of the ambiguous pronoun "they" and placing the attribution last in this passage:
    "He left, returned. The next clerk didn't speak Spanish either.
    "'Why can't *they* learn English?' *she grumbled to me*, the next in line."
    Readers will most likely refer "they" to the clerks and attribute the quotation to Mr. Delgado, until they reach the attribution to the clerk. Ambiguity hurts clarity, but can have meaning.

4) Erwin includes three paragraphs of context: "Delgado, 46,...children to come." Try moving this passage around. No matter where you put context sections, they hurt the flow. Where will it do the least harm and yet come early enough to help the reader's understanding?

5) As she begins her ending, Erwin says, "I was right about Luis Manuel Delgado." I think this transition refers back to her earlier remark to the clerk: "He probably won't.... But maybe his kids will." How could we clarify this sentence so that readers would not get confused and have to guess what she refers to?

6) Is the ending of this piece fair to the clerks? How does Erwin help the reader sympathize with them? Does a columnist have to treat everyone fairly?

His friends recall man of the street

JUNE 29, 1989

The square of sidewalk marred by old bubble gum splotches and a bicycle skid mark in front of Alpha Beta No. 172 in Westminster is unremarkable except that it was kind of a home to Hubert Creasy.

No one knows who put it there, but a handwritten cardboard sign now marks the spot where he sat in recent months:

"IN MEMORY OF THE HOMELESS MAN THAT SAT HERE. HE PASSED ON THIS WEEK. MAY HE REST IN PEACE."

Dorothy Cole, a longtime Westminster resident, saw the sign and remembered Creasy as "a real friendly, nice man."

"I didn't know him really," she said, "but he always had a kind word. Most homeless, well, you know, don't even bother."

She went in the store, bought a 4-inch potted croton, and placed it outside, beneath the sign.

Customers reading the sign appeared to be slightly stunned at first and then shook their heads.

An older woman made clucking sounds with her tongue. "What a pity," Mary Pitkus said. "I bought him some bologna once."

Tanned and stocky, Creasy, 55—a 6-1, 220-pound transient with gray hair and a long beard—endeared himself to people at the corner shopping center with his quick wit and friendly manner.

And although he drank—a lot and often, I'm told—they didn't hold it against him.

He showered at a local motel a few times a week. He used Copenhagen snuff but didn't spit in public. He liked to chat, and sometimes those he spoke to offered him regular jobs, which he never accepted.

"He always helped us with the carts, but didn't want to work regular," said a 24-year-old box girl who considered him a friend.

"He had a bottle of wine in his backpack and

sipped on it all the time. That was his problem. I told him it made him lazy."

A stock girl said she once saw Creasy trim a youngster's hair while her mother shopped inside. The woman paid him with food.

A checker said Creasy helped his favorite customers lift grocery bags into the trunks of their cars. One such customer recently took him shopping for clothes at K mart.

He bought lottery tickets with a customer named Helen, and sometimes spoke of a son and daughter to the box girl.

"Oh, I'm too ashamed to tell them I'm homeless," she recalled him saying when she suggested that he live with one of them.

The son and daughter live in San Diego County, but neither knew much about the man.

"The truth is, I didn't know him at all," the son said. "Something about drinking and bad checks and going to prison. I only remember seeing him once, when I was about 14 years old."

The one person who knew him well, perhaps, was his sister in Waynesboro, Tenn. She is crushed, guilt-ridden, and angry about his death, which was as unglamorous as his life. He died of natural causes while lying in ice plant near a freeway on-ramp.

"There were nine of us kids and we lived a hard life up in the Ozark Mountains," said Shirley Berry, 42. "Lots of times we didn't have anything to eat but oatmeal and no sugar. Maybe that rough start is what did it."

She said he was a skilled carpenter who had new cars and new homes during his life, but "always drank until everything was gone."

Many family members ostracized him, she said, but she accepted him as he was: a guy who loved a good ball game, chocolate pie, fried chicken, and traveling.

She often asked him to come to Tennessee.

"It makes me mad," she said through tears. "Why didn't he come to me? People like him have people who love them, but they're too darn proud.

"He could have had a home. Truth is, I think there was something about that life he liked."

Observations and questions

1) In the first paragraph, Erwin does not identify "Alpha Beta No. 172" as a grocery store. How do we judge when to identify something that everyone knows under a trade name? How do we know what everyone knows?

2) This piece contains lots of closely observed detail. Study each detail to determine what it contributes to its passage, to the whole piece, and to the tone.

3) The sign on the sidewalk reads: "IN MEMORY OF THE HOMELESS MAN *THAT* SAT HERE. HE PASSED ON THIS WEEK. MAY HE REST IN PEACE." Would you be tempted to correct the grammar of the first sentence by substituting *"WHO"* for *"THAT"*? Why? Why not?

4) Dorothy Cole says, "I didn't know him really...but he always had a kind word. Most homeless, *well, you know*, don't even bother." We normally don't even hear fillers like "well" and "you know" when subjects speak them, and we usually delete them from quotations if we do hear them at all. Should we delete "well, you know" from this quotation? Why? Why not?

5) Because of the store's restrictions, Erwin could not name the employees she quoted. Does this lack of specificity hurt the credibility of the story? How could we balance any such loss?

6) Erwin does not give all the named speakers their full identification with address, age, etc. Do columnists have a license to leave some of this apparatus out? Why do we want it in the first place?

7) Erwin never tells why Creasy liked to live on the street. I would like to know why, and I suspect readers would too. How could Erwin find out, and how could she tell readers without speculating or appearing to read minds?

An old flame still burns after 50 years

JULY 6, 1989

For more than 50 years, Ed looked for Katherine wherever he went.

His heart danced in his chest when he passed a woman with dark, auburn hair. He looked for her in their favorite restaurants. Once, he browsed through her favorite dress shop on the pretense of shopping for his mother.

Over the years, the cafes were torn down and the dress shop closed. She was a true love lost.

Few women walked like she walked, a very slight sway, just from the hips down. Sexy in a subtle, honest way.

She had compassion for even the smallest living creature; she hated war and sports.

He remembered her perfume and the way she sipped lemonade. She was partial to chocolate but it never ruined her figure, at least not in the two years Ed knew her.

As he recalls, Katherine had calm blue eyes, a slightly pointed, small nose, and rarely laughed out loud. Her smile was one of those enduring, classic smiles. He is certain it is the same now—even after so many years.

They were in their early 20s then, back in the 1930s. "We were so young and so beautiful," Ed said in his sad, poetic way.

Ed is 73 and retired from government work. His hair is almost gone, he wears baggy pants and lives in a back room of his daughter's home in Anaheim, the city he has lived in for most of his days.

His wife of 37 years died five years ago. He loved her like a wife, faithfully and respectfully. She was great with their four children and cooked darn good Sunday meals. They enjoyed family outings and were active in their church.

But he never felt the same raw, consuming obsession he had for Katherine. He is certain she had the same feelings for him.

"Katherine. Katherine," he said in a whisper. "When my wife was living, I always feared I'd say her name in my sleep."

The last time Ed was with Katherine was on a rainy night in April 1933. The couple had a terrible fight. Ed doesn't recall what they quarreled about, but both being of stubborn nature, neither would apologize first.

The next week, he saw Katherine going into a picture show with a man he despised. He still thinks she accepted the invitation just to spite him.

Later that month, she left town to visit an aunt in Idaho. He never saw her again.

What became of Katherine, I can't say. Ed heard she came back to the area married to a man from Idaho. He heard that she worked in a lawyer's office for a short time and then heard that she had a few kids.

About a year ago, he went with a friend to a church where they play bingo on Wednesdays. Behind the coffee and cake table was a woman with calm blue eyes, a slightly pointed, small nose, and a classic smile.

Ed was almost certain it was Katherine, but he couldn't be sure.

"For years, I had practiced and refined what I would say to her," Ed said. "I was going to remind her about the lovely lace curtains at the cafe. She wanted a kitchen with those curtains.

"I was going to say her auburn hair was just as lovely, but of course, it wasn't auburn anymore.

"I was going to tell her I saw her at the movie house that night.

"And then I was going to tell her what a fool I was letting her go like that."

Ed didn't say any of those things. He never even asked anyone her name.

Instead, he just watched the woman he believes was Katherine and felt angry that he was old and nearly bald and wrinkled.

And when the last bingo number was called, he looked at her one last time and then walked home to his room at the back of the house.

Observations and questions

1) This piece moves back and forth between the past and the present, in and out of Ed's memory, creating problems of chronology. Study how Erwin handles the time scheme. What works, and what might confuse readers?

2) Try rearranging this piece into a straight chronological narrative, perhaps by cutting up a photocopy and moving the pieces around. What effects do you create? Does the clarity improve? How else could you arrange the story?

3) Ed laments a lost era and his lost youth as well as a lost lover. Look for details and phrasing that create this sense of the past. Remember that Erwin had to notice them in her interview.

4) Ed doesn't talk much early in this piece, and Erwin tells us that he speaks "in his sad, poetic way." Should she let him talk more, perhaps earlier, and let readers draw their own conclusions about how he speaks?

5) We learn in the ninth paragraph that Ed is 73 years old. Would it help the reader to move this detail higher? Where would you put it and how?

6) Erwin uses a flashback to tell how Ed lost Katherine: "The last time...He never saw her again." Try moving this passage around for different effects.

7) Let's shorten Erwin's kicker: "And when the last bingo number was called, he looked at her one last time and then walked home to his room at the back of the house." Cover up the following phrases and study the effects produced: "at the back of the house," "to his room at the back of the house," "and then walked home to his room at the back of the house." Which version works best?

Gang killings create cycle of fratricide

SEPTEMBER 18, 1989

Gilbert Nunez is a member of the 17th Street gang. At 20 years old, his street dues are almost paid.

By the time he is 23 or so, he'll be a *veterano*— a veteran of street brawls and shootings. Only then can he leave fighting behind.

As an alumnus of the gang, he'll advise younger members and keep feeding the hatred that fuels the gang's rivalry with the boys from Fifth Street.

Unless he dies first.

And then he'll be a hero to his homeboys—boys from his barrio.

I stood with Nunez outside the house on La Bonita Avenue in Garden Grove where two people died Saturday in what authorities are calling the county's worst drive-by shooting.

The dead—Miguel "Smokey" Navarro, 18, and Frank Fernandez Jr., 4—were Nunez's best friend and his girlfriend's nephew.

Nunez said he and nearly a dozen people were getting into three cars to go to the movies when someone inside the house told him he had a phone call. He was walking toward the front door when the sound of machine-gun fire broke loose.

"I was kissing the dirt," he said. He pointed to a place on the sidewalk that is stained dark red with blood. "The little boy died there."

We leaned on the hood of a candy-apple-red pickup truck and sorted through it all.

He shook his head, and searched for a sensible answer to my question. All I wanted to know was "Why?"

Why do these kids kill one another?

All that separates you from them is Euclid Street, I said. A street.

That street—and the neighborhoods it separates —makes kids kill kids. Hispanics killing Hispanics. *Chicanos, cholos, homeboys, partners.* Call them what you like. It's fratricide.

"Yeah, it's stupid," said Nunez, taking a Camel cigarette from behind his ear and lighting it. "My best friend just got killed over the 'hood (neighborhood). He got shot in my car. I hurt. I hurt inside. We were tights (close)."

Nunez told me the rivalry between youths in the two neighborhoods has been going on since the 1950s. Back then, the 17th Street gang members called themselves the Road Kings. Nunez has a crown tattooed on the outside of his right knee to commemorate the first members.

"My girlfriend's dad was one of the original Road Kings," he said. "Gangs don't stop. There's always another generation. In my generation, more than half are locked up. Some are dead. But we're a family."

I told Nunez that fighting over territory seemed senseless. I was surprised when he agreed.

"I wish we could say, 'That's it. That's enough. Time out,'" he said. "But this is never going to stop."

Why don't you get out? I asked.

"(Expletive), man, you can't get out. This is my 'hood. The young people here, we don't have anything else."

Nunez looked confused for a minute and then pained.

"You know, we had this understanding not to shoot the pads up. Don't mess up my ma's pad, we won't mess up your ma's pad, ya know? We don't shoot when their girls and kids are out there. (Expletive), I don't know what happened."

* * *

A few houses down the street, Rosa Maria Zepeda, 30, stands on the sidewalk in front of her home with friends from the neighborhood.

When the shooting broke out about 7:40 p.m. Saturday, her husband was working under the car in the driveway.

Her brother was walking up the front steps.

"I just hit the ground," said Jesus Magana, 27. "There were bullets flying all over the place."

He pulled a cartridge from his pants pocket that he found by the car where Roberto Zepeda was working.

Rosa Maria Zepeda—a mother of two children, ages 9 and 5—is angry with the Frank Fernandez Sr. family for bringing trouble to the neighborhood.

"It's just this one family," she said. "No one else in this block is in gangs. Just them.

"It's how you're brought up," she said. "I don't even talk to them because what kind of an example would that be for my children? Already they call the little children at that house *cholitos* because their parents dress them like they're from a gang family.

"So I don't mix with them at all.... All of us are now afraid because of one family."

Residents also are angry because an innocent child was killed, and many blame the child's parents—Frank and Irene Fernandez—who they say allow members of the 17th Street gang to congregate at their home.

A foot-high "17" is spray-painted in white on a tree trunk in the family's front yard, and a bench covered with the gang's graffiti sits to one side of the porch.

A man in his 50s wearing khaki shorts, a white T-shirt, and a fishing hat watered his front lawn and acted as if nothing particularly interesting was happening in his neighborhood. A few feet away, news reporters and television crews marched up and down the sidewalk.

"I keep to myself," he said in Spanish. "I don't mix with anyone around here because I don't want any trouble. These kids, their parents don't raise them right. They don't respect anything. Even life."

He said gang members kill their own and don't even know it.

"Today, they'll cry," the man in the fishing hat said. "But tomorrow they'll kill again.

"Crazy."

Observations and questions

1) The first two paragraphs of this story serve as a "nut graph," a short passage that tells readers essential information they must have to understand the rest of the piece. We usually place the nut graph after an anecdotal lead, but here it becomes the lead. Think of alternative ways to start this piece and different placements for the nut graph.

2) Erwin gets Nunez and the shooting firmly onstage before she asks the key question: "Why do these kids kill one another?" Think of alternative places to ask this question, and of other characters in the story who might ask it. What effects would you produce?

3) Erwin quotes Mr. Nunez speaking street lingo: "Yeah, it's stupid.... My best friend just got killed over the *'hood* (neighborhood). He got shot in my car. I hurt. I hurt inside. We were *tights* (close)." Think about the literary gains of using such colorful language, and now think about the problems that quoting non-standard English might cause, especially condescension. How should we balance such gains and losses?

4) Mr. Nunez says, "(Expletive), man, you can't get out." So-called "family newspapers" use all sorts of codes to keep from quoting expletives. Why? What would our readers gain and lose if we just quoted foul language?

5) In the second half of this column, Erwin introduces nine more characters, shifting the focus away from Gilbert Nunez. Would this piece improve by maintaining one central character? We have to make such decisions based on what we actually have in our notes, but we can also predict during interviewing what we may need.

6) The column ends with the word "crazy." The word, image, or thought that comes last controls what readers think about the subject and what they remember. Can you think of a better word than "crazy" to end this piece?

Vets hear new sort of silence at tragic wall

OCTOBER 26, 1989

The air was still until just before midnight.

And then something happened.

Just as the old day expired and the new was born, a slight breeze kicked up and rustled through the trees.

In the center of Chapman College's athletic field at that moment stood a middle-aged man in blue jeans and a plaid flannel shirt. He had been standing in the same spot for quite some time, searching, but just then he reached out and touched a name. His search was over.

There, among the 58,156 names on The Moving Wall—a half-size traveling replica of the Vietnam Veterans Memorial in Washington, D.C.—was the name of a buddy from Vietnam.

The former Marine, now employed by the city of Anaheim, tilted his head back and scrutinized the name for several minutes through bifocals.

He looked to the right and to the left at the dew-covered sea of names, and the enormity of America's longest war hit him.

"Too many names. Too many bodies. Too many souls," he uttered quietly, shaking his head and crying.

He pulled a white handkerchief from his pants pocket and dried his eyes. "What an injustice."

I hugged him a little, awkwardly from one side; I couldn't help it. He thanked me and politely asked if I knew anyone on the wall.

I did not.

I was a young girl when he was a platoon sergeant in Vietnam in '65 and '66. When the peace accord was signed, I was still in eighth grade.

Then why do you care about this? he implored.

I am ashamed, I said. I have always felt ashamed of how returning Vietnam veterans were treated by this country and their countrymen.

I told him I viewed the moral questions as a separate issue.

We forgot, I said, that young men and women abandoned their dreams—momentarily or forever—to serve their nation.

They were products of a John F. Kennedy generation. When he said, "Ask not what your country can do for you; ask what you can do for your country," they believed every word.

I guess America wanted to forget the human tragedy of Vietnam, so we ignored and shunned the memories too. Especially the veterans.

The ungrateful masses, coupled with the horror and trauma of war, left many bitter.

Yes, I said, I am ashamed.

He looked surprised, then resigned.

"Yeah, I really don't try to think about it anymore. It makes me mad."

My answer wasn't as important to him as the fact that someone who wasn't there cared.

It was 1 a.m., and others walked onto the sports field.

Like the veterans' return, there were no cheering crowds, parades, or banners. Just an overwhelming silence.

The silence on the field at Chapman College was different, though, from the one veterans came home to so many years ago.

This time, there was something profound and thankful and humbling in it.

"It's a strange time," another vet said. "At first, we were ignored and despised. Now, the moviemakers want to make us heroes. Bizarre. How can you figure that?"

An hour later, halfway through the list of names, the former platoon sergeant turned to leave.

I asked his name.

His answer was poetic: "These are the names that count, not mine."

The breeze picked up again, caught a small note laid on the grass before the black, ominous-looking memorial, and flipped it over.

"Welcome Home Big Brother," it said. "See you in Heaven."

Observations and questions

1) This column begins with an atmospheric lead. Study each detail in it, noting how Erwin sets a mood without telling the reader too much, especially about the landscape.

2) Erwin never tells what the wall looks like, or what it represents. Can we assume that readers know all that? Compose a nut graph to explain it. Now, where are you going to put your nut graph?

3) After the Marine first speaks, Erwin responds: "I hugged him a little, awkwardly from one side; I couldn't help it. He thanked me and politely asked if I knew anyone on the wall." Should reporters hug their subjects? Traditionally we discourage journalists from participating in the actions they write about. Why? Should that prohibition apply to columnists?

4) After the first third, this piece poses a series of questions. Traditionally journalists object to question leads and question structure on the grounds that "we're in the answer business, not the question business." Do you agree?

5) In the middle of this piece, Erwin delivers a tirade about how Vietnam veterans were treated after the war. Would this long speech play better if someone else had said it? Why does Erwin report it in indirect discourse rather than quoting it?

6) Make a list of all the potential endings in this piece. Try each one out for suitability, remembering that whatever comes last determines the meaning of whatever came before. Do all those potential kickers give the piece a sense of stopping and restarting?

7) This column about names on the wall has no names in it at all, of the dead or the living. Why not?

A conversation with
Diana Griego Erwin

DON FRY: You're second-generation Hispanic, aren't you?

DIANA GRIEGO ERWIN: Well...

Why do you hesitate?

You said "second-generation." The "Griego" name comes from my father's side, from the Spanish settlement days in New Mexico, so we've been here for generations and generations, from the 16th century.

Oops, sorry about that. You're more American than I am!

We do have relatives through intermarriage who are more recently, say, from Mexico. And my mother is a distant relative of President Rutherford B. Hayes. So sometimes I'm a little confused when people try to put labels on me. But I do say I'm Hispanic, because I feel a great affinity for the culture, and an understanding too.

You're the second minority person and the first Hispanic to win this prize. What experiences have you had as a Hispanic in Anglo newsrooms?

It affected me more from outside the newsroom than from inside. You really don't know what kind of fringe people are out there until you write a column with your picture and name on it. The first week I had the column, I got some mail I really wasn't prepared for. I got a piece of cardboard in the mail, and someone had written on it with bold, black marker: "We don't need any more Mexicans in Orange County."

Yike!

That was really shocking to me. "Griego" is not a common name; some people think it's Italian. So I haven't experienced a great deal of bias or bigotry in my life. But in the newsroom, people think of my being Hispanic, and that I speak Spanish, as a benefit.

But I think some of my colleagues try to stay away from me when I'm writing about ethnic issues. I think they feel uncomfortable.

Give me an example.

When I first started, I was getting some really bad mail, really bigoted stuff. So I wrote a column that explained my ancestry. I explained stereotypes, and how we can either believe them and hate one another for them, or we can see past them. I printed parts of one of the letters and answered that letter. No one in the newsroom said anything to me about that column, although a couple of people usually say something about every column. And then a couple of days later, I did another column that irritated a few people in the newsroom, and believe me, they told me about it. So it just gives me the feeling that some folks perhaps don't quite know how to react personally to a colleague's ethnicity.

Did you have similar experiences as a Hispanic at *The Denver Post*?

When I first joined the *Post,* I was the only one who spoke Spanish in the newsroom. It was wonderful. I was a brand-new reporter, and I got to cover the Mexico City earthquake. Denver had about 18 percent Hispanics at the time, and colleagues would say, "I'm really glad we finally have someone around here who can understand Hispanics." I got a lot of letters and calls from the community, and I think the *Post* was able to do a lot of stories that we might not otherwise have been able to do, not because I have such a great understanding, but because the community felt that they could be more open and better understood by someone with the last name Griego.

Did you feel an obligation to cover the Hispanic community?

Not at all. In fact, in the beginning, I didn't do that many stories about the Hispanic community, unless it just came up in the course of something else. Later I became the minority affairs writer, but I also covered blacks and Asians and gays.

I really enjoy explanatory journalism, where you can actually open someone's eyes to something they never thought of before. After the column "His dreams belong to the next generation," I had a couple of people at the *Register* say, "You know, I never thought of it like that before. You really changed the way I feel." And that really makes you feel good as a writer. You really accomplished something.

Indeed. At Poynter, we're trying to get newspapers to explain things, and to redefine news to include coverage of communities different from the newsroom's.

And it's exciting to read about. That's the trick: to describe an experience readers don't know anything about in terms that they can understand, and then to bring them around so that they really have a feeling for what it's like. That's challenging writing, and very satisfying.

How do you do that? Excuse my extreme terms, but how do you explain an alien culture to people who aren't aliens?

Well, I always start out with a story they can read like a novel, and I tell it in great detail, so they can see it, so they can taste it and feel it, and I try to put them there. And then all of a sudden, I hit them with something really strange, what this means to those people, something that readers aren't think-ing about at all.

Good tactic.

And the readers have to stop for a second and won-der, and then I explain some more about why peo-ple think that way, and then I hit them with another story. They need more than one reinforcement for something that is, as you say, that alien. I either doubly reinforce it, or take them to the next step.

How do you know what readers don't know? How do you see something with innocent eyes, so you know what to tell them?

Well, I see a lot of innocent eyes all around me, and mine have been that way before. I grew up in a pretty middle-class upbringing, and I didn't know a whole lot from my own experience about the bar-rio or the ghetto. We have a lot of diverse peoples in Orange County now, people from all over, and in the beginning, I didn't know anything about them. And you just remember the way you felt, and how you came to that understanding.

How do you find such good subjects?

I love to observe people, and I wish there were a career called "professional observer."

It's called "reporter." [Laughter]

But then you have to write it. [Laughter] You can find out so much about people just by watching them. Being a reporter is great, because you can ask people questions that no one in their right mind would ask a complete stranger.

We have a license to be rudely friendly.

Yes. [Laughter] I've always used "friendly." I've had to use "rude" with people who are a little more savvy with the media, but very, very rarely.

Do you take notes in English or in Spanish?

Both. For Spanish speakers, I take them in Spanish.

But you work for an English-language newspaper. How do you handle quotations in Spanish that have to be printed in English?

I quote them in English, and I say, "So-and-so said in Spanish."

Why bother?

Since I change the quotes a little bit from one language to another, I think I need to say that they spoke in Spanish.

Honesty with the reader, perhaps?

Right. Otherwise, it's unfair, and it's inaccurate, even if it's a word-for-word translation.

How do you handle idioms? You can't translate idioms word for word.

Sometimes I let them remain strange-sounding, because it adds a touch that this person comes from another place, or has a different background. Readers want to know more about this person. I don't do it in any way that would make people look foolish or unworldly.

Americans are very prejudiced against non-standard English, even though they don't speak standard English themselves. So quoting any kind of dialect, or anything like dialect, can imply incompetence, ignorance, even inferiority, on the part of the speaker.

Yes, it can, and if it does, I don't use it.

Do you use a tape recorder?

Not as much as I used to. I've learned to take notes quickly. I record people like politicians, or people who might decide that they don't like the way something looks in print, even though they said it that way.

People who might quibble about the quotations....

Right. I write a lot about everyday people, and the message has a more universal truth. There's less risk of those people saying, "You've misquoted me." But my notes are really pretty complete.

How do you know when you have enough? How do you know when to stop reporting and start writing?

I always have three to four times what I use in the column. Many days, I could tell three stories. I don't say that I've done more work than I should have, because all that extra work has given me more understanding of this person or this situation, so I can write feeling that I really know that person. I feel I've gotten inside people and know where they stand.

So how do you know when you have enough?

Oh, I guess when the person's exhausted. [Laughter] I just feel I know the person, and they usually feel the same way about me. I reveal a lot about myself in interviews. It makes people feel comfortable, and it only seems fair to me. That might sound strange, but...

No, that's good interview technique.

That's the way our conversations go, like friends. Even when I'm writing something negative about someone, I'm always honest about the angle of the story.

You tend to interview what journalists call "unsophisticated subjects," as opposed to, say, politicians who are savvy about the media. Do you feel obligated to tell unsophisticated people how things they say might look if you printed them?

I always tell them, "You realize this is going to be in the paper, and it's okay, right?" And with people who've no experience with the media at all, I say something like, "Remember, your wife or your boss is going to read this." I did that just yesterday, in fact.

Do you think that kind of warning inhibits people from saying the things you need them to say?

Well, maybe in the beginning. But by the time we're halfway through the conversation, trust has developed. There are many reasons why people talk to a newspaper. Some people decide it's therapeutic, or some people decide the public needs to know this, or understand them.

Sometimes I wonder why they talk to me, and sometimes I worry the next day, "Are they going to read this and think, 'Oh, no. She actually printed what I said.'" But they never do. They call and say, "You know, you got it just right," or, "You made me think about some things about myself that I hadn't really gotten down to thinking about before."

Just listening to you, I can tell that if *you* interviewed *me*, you would get a lot out of me. At Poynter, we call that "soft interviewing," as opposed to the hard-edged interviewing you see on TV, the Sam Donaldson approach, which is really an attack, not a conversation.

Right.

When you've done all the reporting on a column, how do you organize your materials?

When I'm driving back to the office in the car,

I've already constructed in my head probably the first three paragraphs. Usually halfway through the interview, I hear the lead. But sometimes that changes, because something else comes along and pushes it out of the way. I do a lot of bouncing off a couple of people in my life and here at the newsroom before I sit down to write....

Between the reporting and the writing?

Sometimes I do it even before I go out. In every newsroom, there are people who are specialists in different areas, and I rely a lot on those people for their expertise and knowledge.

Right. What kind of people do you bounce ideas with?

It depends on what I'm writing about. It could be someone who covers politics or courts, if that's the type of column I'm working on, and they know the players. Generally I ask them, "Who can really tell me about this?" or, "Who can provide a history on why things have gotten this way?" Reporters who have covered the beat for a long time know these people.

I call them "pathfinders," people who show you where to go first.

Yes, and I like the way some people think. We can just brainstorm about an idea, which helps me to become more focused. Sometimes you have several thoughts on a particular subject, but in a column, you really need to focus on one thing.

Do you brainstorm with people who are not journalists?

Oh, yes. My husband helps me a lot with ideas. I have a girlfriend who's very up on the news, although she has nothing to do with the news business. I just chat with her. I also bounce ideas off a teacher at a junior high school in Orange County, who has varied interests. Basically, they're people who're up on the news and interested in what's going on in their lives and in their community, but they're not news people. My column does not reflect, I would say, a newsperson's point of view.

Why not?

[Laughs] Well, I prefer to go out into the city or the suburbs, and write about the kinds of things that people are thinking and talking about. I think everyone who works for newspapers sees things from an insider point of view. And so a lot of what I try to do is to represent the common people.

For instance, this last Friday, President Bush was here in town speaking about drugs. And we covered it as a newspaper would and should. We covered the speech, and there were a lot of school-children invited, so we interviewed kids. And I thought, "Well, this is preaching to the choir." So I found a couple of drug dealers and took them to the speech at the stadium...

You did?! [Laughter]

...because I thought, "Well, these are the people who really need to hear this. And I would like to know what they think about this."

What did they say?

Well, one of them got pretty into it. Everyone was doing the "wave" and clapping, and he started doing this stuff too. Whatever Bush would say, he'd start clapping. But the other guy was very cynical. He'd see all the anti-drug signs, and he'd say, "Boy, this is heavy."

[Laughter] Back to technique. What do you do next?

When I get back to the office, I take a legal pad,

and before I even look at my notes again, I start writing two or three words to describe each thought. I write down the things that I absolutely have to get into the piece, really detailed. It might be an anecdote or a quote that stuck out in my mind. I just write these things in no particular order, and start grouping things together, saying, "This will follow this perfectly." I use a very informal outline, and then I start numbering all those things, where they're going to go.

Do you think of the piece as having separate parts? And how many?

Oh, yes. I don't really have a particular number, but I try to do it in as few as possible. I really like three parts to a column: this is the lead, and then this center part, and then this is how I'm going to wrap it all up.

My friend Bill Howarth calls that structure "From, through, to." Then what?

Then I tear that piece of paper off, and make it much more organized. Instead of having all these numbers jumping all over the page on that first rough draft of the outline, I put them in the order that I've numbered them.

How detailed does that outline get?

Not very. Maybe three or four words to describe each thought, but they're in a logical order now. I want to end up with a logical order that I can follow and refer to, especially if I start to stray a little bit.

Then I sit down and put that paper next to my terminal, and I still haven't opened my notebook yet. Then I just start to write, just like that. And when I come to a quote I want to use, I might put "the burro quote."

You don't look it up in the notebook?

Not yet. I just write down what the quote's going to be.

Why don't you look it up?

Because I want to continue this train of thought while I'm writing. Someone told me once, "Just get it down the way you remember it, because that's the way you would tell it if you were telling it to your friend." I do that really fast, and maybe it only takes me about 15 minutes to write the whole thing.

You mean the whole draft.

Yes, it's just a draft. And then I go from beginning to end, and I don't move on to the next part until I have everything perfect in the part I've just finished.

You don't revise at all until you've got a whole draft?

Right. But then I revise that same draft. I don't print that first draft out, and then start all over again. Sometimes I write the ending right after I've written the beginning.

Why do you do that?

Because sometimes I know what I'm going to use for the ending, and it's like another story that really sums up what the column is going to say, and I'm just so excited about getting it down. It also helps me in some columns when I know I need to tailor the middle so it flows right into that ending.

"From, through, to." I usually write the ending first, at least in my head, and I almost always write the lead last. I think of the ending as a target that I'm aiming at, and so I write up to it, and then put a good lead on top.
How long does it take you to revise?

It depends. It takes me probably two or three hours, but not always that long. A lot of that time is because I sit in a really busy section of the newsroom and people around me like to talk a lot. They like to come up and bounce ideas. I think that makes a good newsroom.

So do I. Do you get edited much?

I don't get edited a whole lot, but sometimes my editor comes back to me with suggestions if she's unclear about something, or doesn't think a particular transition works.

Do you know the copy editors at the *Register*?

Only a few work on my column, and I know them mostly over the phone. They call me at night, maybe two or three times a month, and say, "I want to make this one little change." It's just something they think will clarify understanding.

Do they do that with everybody, or just with you? Normally copy editors don't call people up in the night for little changes.

It's an understanding I inherited from the former columnist. But I'm glad that they do that, and I've let them know that I'm really glad about it. We have this rapport, and when they call, I say, for the most part, "Yes, that really does make it better."

Right. I tell my copy editors to call any time they want to talk about anything, because I treasure them. They keep me from making a fool of myself.
 Do you get much feedback on your pieces?

I get a lot of feedback, mostly from the community. I get a lot of mail, and about 20 phone calls a day. I hear more from my newsroom colleagues when they're unhappy with me. There have been a couple of times where I've made people very angry....

Over what?

Oh, I wrote this one column about our impressions
of the homeless, focusing on this one woman whose
whole world had fallen apart because she was unable to work. I wrote something about how most of
us presume the homeless to be drug addicts and al-
coholics. And a few people around here, not the
whole newsroom, were angry with me. A few people said very bitterly that I had reinforced the
stereotype, but in my mind, I was saying this is how
we *view* the homeless.

Well, how *do* you avoid reinforcing stereotypes?

I don't worry too much about stereotyping. Usually in the process of interviewing, I try to get to
know someone very, very well, and when you can
do that, you don't have to fall back on stereotypes.
You don't have to assume things about the person
or their situation. I just try to paint people as they
really are.

**There are two problems with stereotypes. One is
avoiding them in what you write, and the other
is seeing beyond them yourself. How can you
avoid stereotypes in your own head?**

I have gotten to know many people, many different kinds of people, and I don't lump them racially
or socioeconomically. I look at every person as
having his or her own story.

I lived and worked in an orphanage in Mexico
for about a year in a very, very impoverished area.
I think seeing the world in a different way made
me more accepting, and made me understand that
the way I think is not the way everyone thinks.
And so, when I'm reporting, I put myself aside
and try to see the world through this person's eyes,
and present him or her that way to readers.

**Let's talk about some of your pieces, starting
with "His dreams belong to the next genera-**

tion." Was this your idea?

Yes. This was one of my first columns. ...

Whoa! One of your first columns?

Yes. This was the second column I ever wrote.

How long before had you written your first one?

Two days before.

So you won this prize for your first four or five months of columns. You seem to do everything right at the beginning.

[Laughter] Isn't that strange?

Magic perhaps. Go ahead.

I was at the Department of Motor Vehicles, renewing my registration. There was this man several feet in front of me, and I could see that he was troubled at not understanding English, and that he was embarrassed about it. The clerk was too busy for this, and she didn't want to deal with it. I'm sure if I had her job, my patience would be a little short too. I just painted a picture in my own brain. I watched the detail, and looked at the way he looked, and recorded his emotions. At that point, I didn't really know that it was a story. He went and stood next to the wall, where all the other immigrants were, waiting for the translator to come back from lunch. So I did my business, and went over and struck up a conversation with him. When he said the part about the donkey, I knew it was a column.

Let me read you the top:
 "His brow furrowed, and the crow's-feet deepened as he struggled to understand. There was little doubt. He was confused.
 "The busy information clerk at the Department of Motor Vehicles in Santa Ana didn't notice.

"'You need to go over there,' she said, pointing across the room to the sea of people waiting. 'I already told you.'

"It was 11 a.m. Her patience was shot for the morning.

"The man pulled at the waistband of his beige work pants and scratched his sun-aged face. He stared at her, stalling for time as he tried to understand, but afraid to say he didn't.

"He left, returned. The next clerk didn't speak Spanish either.

"'Why can't they learn English?' she grumbled to me, the next in line.

"'He probably won't,' I said. 'But maybe his kids will.'"

That's a long, anecdotal lead.

Yes, very long.

You wait until the sixth paragraph to tell the reader about the language problem: "The next clerk didn't speak Spanish either." Why did you hold that detail so long?

Sometimes if you start off right away saying that the language is the problem, readers won't go on. Some people are turned off by that. I wanted them to start wondering what was wrong with this man, what his trouble was, to pull them into the story, and get to know him a little bit. They could start to see him, with his work pants, and so on....

I not only can see him, I can also empathize with him. Then you bring in your own father:

"I had to say it. My father had been one of those kids. The ones who learn English although their parents speak Spanish at home. Schools back then didn't offer special programs; some people have told me that nuns rapped their knuckles with a ruler if they spoke Spanish— even on the playground. They learned English quickly and well that way."

That's the way things were back then. In fact, my sister and I didn't learn Spanish at all, other than to hear it when we'd go over to our relatives' house....

You didn't speak Spanish at home?

Not at all, because my father didn't want us to have the same experience. I know many, many Hispanics who are like that. They don't speak the language at all, because their parents said, "You don't need that." It was something negative hanging over you the rest of your life, the parents thought.

A little later, you give the reader three paragraphs of context:
   "Delgado, 46, said he works long hours and doesn't leave in time to attend adult English classes.
   "He came to the United States in 1973 because two brothers and three uncles had migrated here and found better lives than the ones they left in Mexico.
   "Delgado worked as a bricklayer and saved enough moncy so his wife and two children could join him after 2-1/2 years. An uncle paid for the other two children to come."
   Most writers think of context as interrupting the flow of the story, so the problem is always where to put it. How do you decide where it goes?

I try to put it at the place where readers start to become curious about who this guy is. Now, at this particular place, he has just said that he should know how to speak English, but he doesn't have time. At this point, readers might say, "Oh, this guy's just making excuses." Or they might wonder, "How long has he been here? And why doesn't he speak it?" So I try to put context where that question comes up, and that way it doesn't break the flow. And if you don't fill in the background now, their minds wander.

I try to put it just *before* readers start wondering

about it. That way, I look like a genius: I can read their minds.

[Laughter] That's right. But if you put it too soon, they might not want to know about him yet.

Indeed. I don't ever let my reader wonder, because wondering readers aren't paying attention. As you said, their minds wander.

Right.

Toward the end, you have a lot of donkey references: "like a donkey," "*como un burro*," "not a donkey," "will never be donkeys," and the last words: "This is donkey work." Is all that repetition deliberate?

Yes. I'm doing that to reinforce this image Delgado has in his mind of what he *isn't,* and of what he doesn't want his kids to be, and of how he views the job of these people who work at the DMV. And also, I wanted to remind readers that all this was in Spanish. It's a very common phrase in Spanish, and readers unfamiliar with Spanish would learn that. So repetition reinforces how he speaks and the problem of language.

Right. And the phrase "*como un burro*" won't give readers problems, except that you hope some overzealous copy editor won't insert: "(a common phrase in Spanish)."

[Laughter] That's right. That's right.

Let's look at your kicker:
    "He nodded toward the stressed-out information clerks busily shuffling papers behind the government-issued desk. 'And they won't work here,' he said. 'This is donkey work.'"
    How did you come up with that wonderful ending?

He just laid that quote down on a platter in front of me. Because I'd been through this whole thing with Mr. Delgado, I had to bring readers back to the scene. And it was the easiest way of doing that.

Did you spot that quotation as the kicker during the reporting?

Yes. We went on talking a little while longer, but as soon as I heard that, I was pretty certain it was the ending.

When I hear something that good, I'm ready to rush back to my laptop.

[Laughter] That's right. But I always sit and chit-chat. You can give people the creeps if they say something great, and then all of a sudden, you say, "Okay, see you later."

Right. [Laughter] Do you take this last paragraph as a form of poetic justice?

Certainly. Very rarely in everyday conversation do people say things that are just so perfect. He was proud of what he was doing, even though he knew these people saw him as a nothing. He knew that his kids were not going to be like these people who were looking down on him; his kids were going to do better in life. And it was just more than fair to give him this moment of pride. In that last paragraph, readers would view him differently.

In fact, someone I didn't even know here at the newspaper came up to me and said that their mind had been totally changed about people speaking only Spanish by this. It really wasn't by me; it was by Luis Manuel Delgado that it was changed.

Speaking through you. We could say that last paragraph is the revenge of the oppressed.

It is. This column dispelled a little bit of the stereotype about Spanish-speaking people. If it could do that, just a little bit, just in a few heads, then I was happy with it. Over many years, I've had many arguments with people about the Spanish-speaking community, and about people who don't speak English. So it was an important one for me to do.

Who is the audience for this piece?

The audience is English speakers. I want them to leave it feeling more open to the people they see walking down the street, who are different from themselves, but who think in the same way. Like them, this guy wants his kids to get ahead. He wants them to be successful, and have professions where they can provide for themselves. He wants them to speak English. And I don't think anyone would fault him for that, after reading this.

Right. Let's talk about "An old flame still burns after 50 years." You met this guy.

Yes. I met this man at a senior citizens' meeting, and he was a real Don Juan, but just...you know, all talk. And it was very cute the way he was teasing the single older women at this meeting. So I said, "Boy, you certainly have a lot of girlfriends here," and we just got to talking. The next thing I know, he's whispering to me about what had happened to him a short time before, about going to this bingo game. So I had him tell me the whole story, and it made me see older people in a much different way. We forget that they were young at one time, and that they have all of our experiences, plus some. And I just thought this was a lovely story, but, to tell you the truth, I had a hard time getting it printed....

Why?

Well, it lacks a strong point of view, and it lacks a nut graph. My editor said, "We need you to tell us, what does this mean? You know, what are you trying to tell us here?"

Your editor wanted you to preach.

They wanted me to say something like, "We need to see the elderly..." But I think that a column has room for different types of writing from time to time. That doesn't mean you should do a piece like this every week, but I'd like to do a piece like this a few times a year. I just thought readers could go away from it thinking, "You know, that was just a really nice story. Very bittersweet, but..." That's what I hoped.

Technically speaking, the hard thing about writing this piece is keeping the time scheme straight for the reader. Did you think about that at all?

Yes. I take readers by the hand, really, from one section to the next. The first seven paragraphs are all 50 years ago; and then in the eighth, I start to bring them back to the present. I say, "They were in their early 20s then, back in the 1930s." Then you have Ed speaking in the present: "We were so young and so beautiful." Then, still in the present: "Ed is 73 and retired from government work." And so on. It was just very logical to me, because Ed and I talked about it in this order, except we started with the bingo.

Did you consider doing it chronologically?

You mean, starting from 50 years ago?

Just start with the flashback....

And then they would have fought, and then she left town, and then.... Well, then you get to Ed too late, who he is, and what he looks like now. I felt the readers needed to know him by then.

Because it's about him, not about the relationship.

Right.

Right. I want to talk about description. In general, journalists are not very good at describing people physically. Look at the passage beginning in paragraph four:

"Few women walked like she walked, a very slight sway, just from the hips down. Sexy in a subtle, honest way.

"She had compassion for even the smallest living creature; she hated war and sports.

"He remembered her perfume and the way she sipped lemonade. She was partial to chocolate but it never ruined her figure, at least not in the two years Ed knew her.

"As he recalls, Katherine had calm blue eyes, a slightly pointed, small nose, and rarely laughed out loud. Her smile was one of those enduring, classic smiles."

Talk about the reporting for that descriptive passage.

Well, I just talked to him a long time about the things he remembered about her, asking the kind of questions you ask, like: "How was she different from other women you knew?" And one thing he talked about was her walk. I just keep prodding, "Well, what do you mean, 'It was sexy'?" And he says, "Well, not sexy like, you know, where people would think she was a tramp." And then I would ask, "Well, what was sexy about it?" It's funny. You can get into conversations with people you've just met about the things they wouldn't talk about to their best friend.

And you did a composite because he didn't say this as a unit.

No, he didn't. Probably 50 questions about her ended up as this composite. Another thing I do a lot is describing back to people what they're saying.

Talk about that.

I describe things back to them, in their words, but put more the way I'm planning to write it, because I want to make sure that what I'm hearing is exactly what they mean. He told me about the lace curtains at the cafe. I said, "Now, is that the cafe where you used to go? Was that near the dress shop?" I always talk them back, because it's so easy to get things wrong.

Right. Right.

Because you suppose it might be one way, or it might be linked to what they said in the sentence before, when it's not. People dart around. I'm not explaining this very well....

Now, I want to ask you a metaphysical question. When Ed's telling you about the woman he saw and didn't dare to approach because he thought it might be Katherine...

Yes?

Do you think it really was Katherine?

I do.

Why do you think that?

Because he seemed to think it was her. He didn't want to come out and admit it, but there was just something about him that made me think it was Katherine, and I think someone who knew her as well as he did would know. And, to tell you the truth, I was hoping that Katherine would call me.

[Laughter] The power of the press indeed.

I was just hoping that Katherine, or someone who knew her, would call me, but no one did.

Yes, and tell you she's spent her whole life looking for Ed.

[Laughter] Or whatever.

Look, you only get poetic justice in the end of a column, not in real life. [Laughter] This ending is very sad.

Yes, it's pretty sad, isn't it? But this whole dream about Katherine is a sad dream, so it had to be a sad ending.

You and I could think up a corny ending, like, "He'll go on looking for her as the years pass..." or something like that.

I didn't want to be corny though. I didn't want to dismiss this flame he was carrying. I simply wanted to acknowledge it.

Was this "Gang killings" piece your idea?

Well, this is a deadline piece, and it wasn't even my regular day to write. I don't usually write on Mondays.

Why did you?

Because there had been a gang shooting, and officials were calling it the worst ever in Orange County, so I just called in and asked, "Do you want me to write something?" For a while, when I first started writing columns, I would do this frequently. Now we have a second Metro columnist, so I don't really have that liberty.

What were you trying to do in this piece?

I'm trying to say how dumb it is, but I let the gang member say that himself, and also that these are young, Hispanic boys killing other young, Hispanic boys. I was trying to really press one of them to give us a reason why they do this, and, of course, he couldn't. I had talked to him for a long, long time, and just pressed and pressed for an answer, until finally, he said, "Yeah, it's stupid." And in the very last part of the column, you have neighborhood people, people who are the grandparents of kids like these kids, saying, "Yeah, it's crazy." And the man says at the very end, "Today, they'll cry. But tomorrow they'll kill again." I wanted readers who aren't in gangs, who don't know anything about gangs, which is obviously the majority of people, to be able to become an insider and meet one of these kids. But then, it might have been written for the gang members themselves.

Gang members read your column?

They read this one.

How do you know?

Well, they called me. The family where the gang shooting took place was very upset. They said that, by my describing the house, I implied that the parents and the grandparents approved of gang membership. And I said, "Well, you do allow it to happen there. You do allow the kids to congregate there." And they said, "We really can't do anything about that. These are our kids, and we don't know if their friends are in gangs." And I said, "Oh, come on."

Those are parents calling you, not gang members....

This Gilbert Nunez called me back too, and he told me that some of his friends were giving him problems for saying it's stupid. But he wanted to know if I wanted to do some kind of a follow-up. You have to be really careful writing about gang kids, because you don't want to give them publicity to go out and do something else.

Indeed. You also don't want to get them killed.

That's right. But his friends were harassing him more than anything else.

How did you find these gang members?

Well, I just went out to the street where it happened, and I knew where the house was, and that the family would be coming back soon to the home, at least I hoped they would. I interviewed a lot of people on the street, in the churches, just in case I had to go with another idea. I didn't know for sure that this kid was in a gang, but I probably talked to 20 people that day. And by the time I got to him, and he started saying, "Yeah, he was my best friend" and all that, I knew I had something good.

This guy, I guess, is 20 years old. He's not a teen-ager by the way we define teens in the paper, but he is. We were leaning on this red pickup truck, and I kept wondering, "Is this other gang going to come by here and start shooting it up again?" [Laughter]

Were you afraid?

I was, a little bit. But I thought, "The last thing they're going to do is come to this neighborhood with the cops all around. It's probably the safest place in Orange County today."

[Laughter] Were you afraid *of Gilbert*?

No, I wasn't afraid of him at all. I don't know why. When people can see you as a real person, and you're there taking the time to talk to them, they won't feel intimidated by you, and won't try to scare you or harass you.

I find him very human, at least the way you present him.

Well, he was.

You did this on deadline. Did you write this one faster than normal?

Oh yes, a lot faster.

How long did it take you from the end of re-porting until you turned it in?

Probably about 45 minutes.

How did you plan it, so you could write it that fast?

I think I just sat down and wrote. On deadline, that's what I do. And then I move things around a lot. I write some columns in my head. I think of them as telling a story, as if I called you on the phone and said, "Don, guess what happened to-day." Then I would tell you the nut, and then I'd say, "I met this guy named Gilbert Nunez, and he's a member of the 17th Street gang, and he's only 20 years old, but..." I think a column is often told best that way.

As conversation.

Yes.

Last question. You won the Pulitzer Prize in your first year, and then you won the ASNE award as a fairly new columnist. What are you going to do next?

I'm just going to keep writing. I love the writing part as much as the reporting part, and this is the only thing I know how to do. I've had some other jobs in my life, but this isn't like work. Not to say that it isn't hard and challenging, because it is. But I enjoy it so much.

Working for a newspaper is a kick, ain't it?

I think so, and sometimes journalists tend to forget that. There's a lot of complaining in newsrooms, and cynicism about the whole business. But when you think about it, how many people have as much fun at work as we do?

Samuel Francis
Editorial Writing

SAMUEL FRANCIS's selection in 1989 for an ASNE Distinguished Writing Award was a special treat for *The Washington Times,* a paper that is usually overshadowed by *The Washington Post.* Francis's selection for the same award in 1990 is confirmation that his editorial writing is second to none. He was born in Chattanooga, Tenn., and earned a bachelor's degree from Johns Hopkins University in 1969. He earned a master's and a doctorate in history from the University of North Carolina at Chapel Hill. Francis worked at the Heritage Foundation for four years and in the U.S. Senate as a staff aide for five years before turning to journalism at *The Washington Times*, a newspaper owned by the Unification Church.

Justice reborn

JANUARY 26, 1989

When 2,000 volts of lightning slammed into the body of Ted Bundy Tuesday morning, America suddenly became a little bit cleaner and a little bit safer. For nearly a decade, the notorious serial killer had exhausted his fertile imagination in exploiting every conceivable legal and public relations maneuver to avoid execution. But neither the ingenuity of Bundy and his lawyers, the pedantry of judges, nor the lachrymose quackery of death penalty opponents could stop this week's grim ceremony in Florida's death house. The killer's progress to the hot seat was met with the cheers of citizens impatient that justice be done.

The nation's pundits, for the most part, have not yet weighed in, but the more courageous opponents of the death penalty may soon wax solemn about the viciousness of capital punishment and the ghoulishness of those who celebrated Bundy's death. With celebrants brandishing frying pans, wearing "Burn Bundy" T-shirts, and guzzling beer and doughnuts outside the Florida prison, what seems to have developed into the social event of the season may well have gone too far.

Yet most of those who exuberated over the execution were not ghouls, and their conduct ought to tell us something worrisome about what many decent people have come to believe about the state of criminal justice in the United States. The visitation of strong punishment upon criminals clearly known to be guilty is regarded as unusual, and when it occurs many citizens consider it the exception rather than the rule and the occasion for making merry.

Some may sermonize that Bundy's death will not restore to life any of his victims, and they will fallaciously equate his own death with those he caused. Yet nothing that the state of Florida did to this creature at all resembled what he did to his victims. Florida's executioner did not lacerate Bundy's face and hands with a hacksaw as he admitted he did to the body of 18-year-old Georgann Hawkins. It did not beat him to death with the branch of a tree or leave toothmarks on his corpse as he did to the bodies of two sorority coeds. It did not rape him, kill him, and pitch his corpse into a pigsty as he did to 12-year-old Kimberly Leach of Lake City, Fla. None of these victims will be resurrected because Bundy is now dead, but then, no more will go to their graves because of him either, and the ghosts of the young women he hunted will now perhaps be stiller.

Bundy's execution was the occasion for much biographical wallowing: He was born out of wedlock, his father remains unknown, his grandfather was violent, he early showed the signs of "sociopathic" behavior. Some will seize on these factoids to argue that he was not morally responsible and that therapy, not punishment, was the "proper" way to deal with him. But to deny even Ted Bundy his moral responsibility, and the rewards and punishments that responsibility obliges, is to deny the very concept of what is proper. If human beings are not responsible for their actions, then there is nothing "proper" to be done with any of us. Justice, even in a black leather hood at dawn, is kinder and gentler, more merciful and more humane, than the pseudoscience that seeks to replace it.

Ted Bundy died because he deserved to die. Some of the admittedly tasteless celebrations of his death recognized this truth, but they also were hailing its recognition by those public authorities who sent Bundy to his fate. For years many of our leaders have been blind to this truth, and if they now are beginning to grasp it more firmly, that is cause for celebration.

Observations and questions

1) Editorials are often thought to be strong on cerebral appeals rather than visual appeals. Pick any two paragraphs in this editorial and note the visual images evoked by the writing. What are the effects of this type of writing?

2) Is this editorial fair to Bundy, to the crowd at the execution, to opponents of the death penalty? Should an editorial be fair? Why?

3) Samuel Francis said he doesn't hesitate to use "big words" because he thinks readers are brighter than they're assumed to be, or if they don't know the term, the editorial will challenge them to check a dictionary. What are some of the unexpected or difficult terms used in this editorial? Can readers decipher them from the context in which they are presented? How can writers use unfamiliar terms without losing readers?

4) Often writers start a piece with a strong lead, then the writing sags. Francis's strongest paragraph is the lead, but the rest of the editorial is also compelling. What are major points or devices in each paragraph that sustain your interest in the editorial?

5) A pivotal sentence in the editorial says: "Justice, even in a black leather hood at dawn, is kinder and gentler, more merciful and more humane, than the pseudoscience that seeks to replace it." What is the "pseudoscience"? Is the meaning of the sentence clear? Analyze the emotional appeals in the sentence.

Bush's uncertain verses

FEBRUARY 24, 1989

The race is on to find out whether Salman Rushdie's pen is mightier than the Ayatollah Khomeini's sword. The author of *The Satanic Verses* has withdrawn to the bunkers to save his scalp from pious Moslems entering the Iranian version of LottoAmerica: The ayatollah is offering a grand prize of $5.2 million to any Son of the Prophet who brings him Mr. Rushdie's head on a platter. He's also offering nearly half that sum to any infidel who bags the blasphemer first.

Meanwhile, the Western world's literati have strapped on sword and buckler to do battle with the heathen. Across the country literary notables have organized rallies and public readings from Mr. Rushdie's offensive novel in protest of the ayatollah's bounty hunters. For a decade Iran's violent messiah has nurtured murder and mayhem through out the Middle East and against U.S. citizens and diplomats, but only when he set his gunsights on a member of the international literary brotherhood did the savants begin to sweat.

Intellectuals, of course, cannot be expected to offer a more strenuous response to the ayatollah's terrorism than the gestures from which they make their living. But governments and their leaders ought to do more. While 12 European states have defiantly slapped Iran's First Lunatic in his face by pulling their diplomats out of his country, President Bush and Secretary of State James Baker have merely stuck out their tongues.

After a week of silence in the wake of the ayatollah's blustering, Mr. Bush this week denounced it in a reply to a reporter's question. He expressed support for the European Community's declaration against Iran, defended Mr. Rushdie's right to publish his book and the publishers' right to sell it, and proclaimed that "inciting murder and offering rewards for its perpetration are deeply offensive to the norms of civilized behavior."

But Mr. Bush did not go so far as to say exactly what should or would be visited upon the ayatollah and his country if U.S. citizens were harmed or their rights violated. "Our position on terrorism is well-known. In the light of Iran's incitement, should any action be taken against American interests, the government of Iran can expect to be held accountable." Mr. Baker hastened to assure the House Foreign Affairs Committee that the United States has no plans to do anything except condemn the Iranian death threat.

But the president's vague and anticlimactic statement will do little to set the ayatollah's mental wheels in reverse, nor will it deter either the avaricious or the pious from cashing in on Teheran's blood money. "Our position on terrorism" is not well-known even in the U.S. government, let alone in Teheran. Sometimes we retaliate; often we don't. Sometimes we declare war against terrorists; sometimes we send them chocolate cakes, Bibles, and TOW missiles.

To say that we will hold Iran's government "accountable" can mean anything from including it in the next published list of states that support international terrorism to dispatching its assassins and their masters on a one-way trip to the Garden of Paradise. Mr. Bush may know precisely what he intends to do, but if so, he has conspicuously failed to impart his knowledge to those who need to hear about it—the ayatollah himself and those who may be considering taking advantage of his generosity.

The Western world has put up with the ayatollah's savagery for 10 years, and the United States in particular has suffered his attack on our embassy and a series of terrorist brutalities masterminded by his mullahs. Nothing we have done in the last decade has succeeded in communicating to him and his cohorts that his contempt for us and his crimes against us will cause him and his people any discomfort they are unwilling to pay. Mr. Bush needs to kick off his administration's response to the ayatollah's overt terrorism with a stronger and clearer message than the one he sent this week. If he doesn't, he might as well pick out his favorite chapter of Mr. Rushdie's book and sign up with the eggheads at the public readings.

Observations and questions

1) This editorial begins with a fast-paced, hip style that gives few details on the background of the situation. Why does this method work? Under what circumstances can the writer jump right in and run with a piece without giving a lot of background?

2) Francis says: "For a decade Iran's violent messiah has nurtured murder and mayhem throughout the Middle East and against U.S. citizens and diplomats..." Does the cynical tone detract from the argument?

3) President Bush is paraphrased and quoted; then portions of the quotes are used to undermine Bush's positions. Why not just disagree with Bush instead of using the president's words? What are the dangers in using partial quotes to belittle the speaker's arguments?

4) The tone of this editorial shifts from flippant narrative to smooth rhetorical development of a position. When does the shift occur? How does the writer manage the transition without an abrupt change? Why is the shift in tone necessary?

5) Sometimes when the writer tries to tie the kicker, or ending, to a reference made early in the writing, the stretch is too great to be meaningful. What happens here? Is it important for the kicker to refer to "eggheads at the public readings"? The "eggheads," or intellectuals, have not been mentioned since the third paragraph.

Hypocrisy on the right?

AUGUST 3, 1989

Many conservatives had themselves a good chortle over Chappaquiddick this summer, 20 years after Sen. Ted Kennedy's blunderous negligence cost the life of Mary Jo Kopechne. They also smirked themselves silly over the Jim Wright scandal, the resignation of Democratic Whip Tony Coelho, and the macabre story of Mr. Wright's aide, John Mack. But while conservatives were busy congratulating themselves on the moral weaknesses of their opponents, some of the floorboards under their own virtuous feet seemed to be caving in. For some reason, many otherwise serious folks on the political right don't seem to get the joke.

First, Ohio's conservative Rep. Donald E. "Buz" Lukens was convicted of having sex with a minor and sentenced to 30 days in the pokey. But Mr. Lukens's escapades pale before the bizarre career of Quentin C. Crommelin Jr., who barely avoided a 10-year prison term for sexual battery.

Crommelin, who seems to be the right's answer to John Mack, served several conservative chiefs on Capitol Hill for many years—the late Sen. Jim Allen of Alabama and John East of North Carolina, Sens. Strom Thurmond on the Senate Judiciary Committee and Jesse Helms on the Foreign Relations Committee. Just about everywhere Crommelin went, however, lurid stories of sexual harassment, violence, and rape seemed to follow him. The tales caught up with him this spring, when a former employee of the Foreign Relations Committee charged that Crommelin had sexually assaulted and kidnapped her. After the usual courtroom bargainings, he pleaded guilty to aggravated sexual battery. A 10-year prison sentence was suspended on condition Crommelin seeks psychiatric counseling.

The Crommelin and Lukens cases are not the only ones involving conservatives. Reps. Bob Bauman, John Hinson, and Dan Crane—all leading lights of the right in Washington—had their political lamps put out by floundering in sexual swamps of their own making. Then there's Jim Bakker, professional conservative Bible-thumper who wound up thumping mattresses with some of his flock. The Craig Spence scandal seems to implicate a number of Republican stalwarts, including one of *The Washington Times*'s own editors.

Of course, none of these scandals on the right proves that conservatives "are just as bad" as liberals, or vice versa. What it does prove is that human nature is the same, regardless of which side of the political fence it favors. But many conservatives seem reluctant to acknowledge this, and few have come forward to denounce the mote in their own side's eye.

This week columnist John Lofton of *The Washington Times* interviewed Mr. Helms about the Crommelin case, and to his credit, Mr. Helms forthrightly read Crommelin out of his precincts. "I find this guy repulsive.... I have no use for him." But two of Mr. Helms's close advisers, Tom Ellis and Carter Wren of the National Congressional Club, were far more circumspect, as are many of Crommelin's associates on the right. "I viewed it as normal behavior of an active bachelor," says one of Crommelin's buddies on Foreign Relations. "I don't have the facts at this point," says Mr. Wren.

But the world and the court have the facts, and if conservative leaders pretend they don't see them, the world will judge them less mercifully than the court judged Crommelin. If conservatives, whose political agenda includes respect for the simple virtues of the Judeo-Christian tradition, don't treat the crooks and perverts among them at least as uncompromisingly as they treat Mr. Kennedy and Mr. Wright, that judgment will be to laugh them out of office as hypocrites and opportunists who haven't earned the right to be taken seriously.

Observations and questions

1) Five characters are introduced in the lead of this piece. Two others are mentioned in the next paragraph. Does the reader get lost in names? How is Francis able to avoid that?

2) The first sentence refers to people who "chortle" over an event 20 years ago in which a woman died because of "blunderous negligence." Is such a heavy lead justified? Does the writer run the risk of making light of a grave situation?

3) Allusions to literature frequently appear in Francis's writing. Here he says: "...few have come forward to denounce the mote in their own side's eye." What is the source of the allusion? What rewards do such references provide for readers?

4) One could argue that this editorial simply says there are as many unsavory conservatives as liberals. Where does the writer raise the argument to a more significant level? Where is the nut graph, or main point of the piece?

5) Francis moves to the conclusion of the editorial by quoting a conservative adviser: "'I don't have the facts at this point,' says Mr. Wren.

"But the world and the court have the facts, and if conservative leaders pretend they don't see them, the world will judge them less mercifully than the court judged Crommelin."

Notice the ways in which the sentences tie together and also tie the arguments of the editorial together.

Rapping garbage as 'art'

AUGUST 24, 1989

"Realistic" is the thing to be these days, especially in art. The late Robert Mapplethorpe was "realistic" with his photographs of sodomy and less nameable practices, and last week our David Mills reported on the "realism" of rap music. The lyrics of some rap groups seem to wallow in not-too-critical descriptions of violence, drugs, and sexuality, all in the name of the realities of life for urban blacks. The rappers, say police, parents, and pundits of pop culture, encourage and even incite mayhem.

Whether violent lyrics spark actual violence is one side of the rap record, but there's another that no one hears. The real question about rap, especially the hard-core variety, is whether it says anything worth listening to.

The storm swells over the lyrics of a song called "F--- the Police," performed by a group known as N.W.A., which is said to stand for "Niggers With Attitudes." "F--- the Police" contains such gems of prosody as

Without a gun and a badge, what you got?
A sucker in a uniform waitin' to get shot
By me, or another nigger
And with a gat, it don't matter if he's smaller or
    bigger

You've got to admit it's not Rodgers and Hammerstein. In fact, it's barely Mother Goose. But aside from the metrical wheelchairs in which rap moves, the excuse rappers give for their artistic accomplishments is that they're just reflecting reality.

"We call ourselves underground street reporters," says N.W.A.'s Ice Cube. "If everybody did records and all we talked about was the joys of life, and on TV all they showed was rainbows and pastel colors, a kid could go out and get his head blown off and not know why." Rapper "Schooly D" Weaver offers perhaps the most decrepit excuse of the mediocre artist. He says he's expressing "the inner me" and "I write exactly what I feel."

But kids can get their heads blown off and still not know why, even after submerging themselves in Ice Cube's limp doggerel. The rappers' vision of reality is simply vicious. They manage to miss the inner city's other realities—family members working for each other, students trying to elevate themselves, community leaders risking their lives to control the garbage rappers celebrate. The rappers have nothing to say about why the garbage is there, how to clean it up, or even why it stinks—because garbage is all they see and all they want their audiences to see.

Great art always reports on reality. It never disguises it, but neither does it ever surrender to it by merely vomiting up only the ugliness that reality contains. No one will much care about the "inner me" of Schooly D and his buddies if all that's inside them is the ugliness they brag about and all that comes out is the artistic equivalent of diarrhea. After their novelty wears thin, they'll be about as enduring as The Beatles' soup-bowl haircuts in the early '60s.

Observations and questions

1) In the lead Francis says: "The rappers, say police, parents, and pundits of pop culture, encourage and even incite mayhem." Does the alliteration stand out as you read it? The use of this device is not pronounced, but it punches up the writing. Writers often ignore opportunities to brighten their writing in small ways.

2) The lyrics of N.W.A.'s song, indeed even the title of the song, raise questions of taste because of the use of profanity, and questions of propriety because of the message. Would you have included the lyrics? What are the arguments for and against including them?

3) Francis says: "You've got to admit it's not Rodgers and Hammerstein. In fact, it's barely Mother Goose. But aside from the metrical wheelchairs in which rap moves, the excuse rappers give for their artistic accomplishments is that they're just reflecting reality." The paragraph takes a shot at rappers, but could other groups find it offensive? Explain.

4) Consider the use of garbage as a metaphor in this piece. What is the garbage? Is the writer successful in following through on the use of the metaphor?

5) Many of Samuel Francis's editorials end with a tie to opening paragraphs. This one ends with a new element, Beatle haircuts, offering a surprise. Is the ending effective?

Urine the money

SEPTEMBER 14, 1989

North Carolina's Sen. Jesse Helms may not look much like Jesus Christ, but some of America's artists have done him the honor of putting him in the same place they put the Man from Galilee. This summer in Phoenix, an "alternative" art center called the MARS Artspace displayed as an exhibit a photograph of Mr. Helms immersed in a Mason jar of the urine of an artist known only as "Cactus Jack." The MARS Artspace, it turns out, is funded by the National Endowment for the Arts—in other words, by you and your tax dollars.

Of course, Cactus Jack, whoever he is, didn't mean to honor Mr. Helms. His creation was a spin-off of artist Andres Serrano's "Piss Christ," a photograph of a crucifix submerged in Mr. Serrano's own liquid offal. That creation too was funded by $15,000 from the NEA, and Mr. Helms's response to what he considered a blasphemous use of the taxpayers' money and a waste of human waste was to sponsor legislation cutting off public funds for obscene and indecent artworks.

MARS art director Jason Sikes says his "immediate reaction" to Cactus Jack's inspiration "on a personal level was that it was hilarious.... My second reaction was that if we put it up, it could cause us problems." Even "alternative" artists have to eat and pay the rent, you see, and even as he was chuckling over how clever Cactus Jack's *piece de resistance* was, Mr. Sikes was beginning to worry whether the yokels might get fed up with him and his whole stupid center.

In the event, Mr. Sikes proceeded with the display and kept it on exhibit until Aug. 17, despite protests from philistines who just don't appreciate genius and clearly have no sense of humor. "We decided," proclaims Mr. Sikes valiantly, "an artist's freedom of expression was more important." But

the belly laugh Mr. Sikes and his friends may have
gotten from their calculated insult to Mr. Helms
may cost them. Rep. Sidney Yates, chairman of the
subcommittee that reviews NEA funding, says he
doesn't think it's funny when artists make sport
with members of Congress. "I don't think any
member of Congress should be treated like that,"
says Mr. Yates of Cactus Jack's masterpiece.

Actually, a good many members of Congress
probably deserve treatment far worse than even
Cactus Jack's morbid imagination could conceive.
It's ironic that at the same time many members of
America's freeloading artistic establishment are furious because taxpayers are getting bored with
picking up the check for the insulting, obscene,
and blasphemous junk that artists create, many
members of Congress also are furious that Americans are growing tired of congressional pomposity,
hypocrisy, and outright corruption. It seems to be
fine with Mr. Yates if whacked-out aesthetes smear
their bodily fluids over mainstream American beliefs and values, but they better not even think about
poking fun at congressmen.

The Senate was right to pass Mr. Helms's amendment. Cactus Jack's micturitions ought to be carried
to the nearest sewer. The Mason jar can serve to
hold Mr. Sikes's income after Congress transfers his
gallery to the free marketplace of ideas. And American taxpayers ought to put Mr. Helms's picture on
their mantels for his courage in pushing an arrogant
gang of parasites off the public dole.

Observations and questions

1) Readers expect most editorials to be plodding, stodgy treatises. This editorial begins with the headline "Urine the money," and a lead that compares the looks of Jesse Helms and Jesus Christ. Few sections of a newspaper could offer readers livelier fare.

2) A tenet in journalistic writing is to identify unfamiliar characters who are mentioned in stories. Francis does the opposite in this editorial. He refers to Cactus Jack as "whoever he is." Why does that approach work? Could it work in news stories?

3) Francis rips MARS art director Jason Sikes in this sentence: "Even 'alternative' artists have to eat and pay the rent, you see, and even as he was chuckling over how clever Cactus Jack's *piece de resistance* was, Mr. Sikes was beginning to worry whether the yokels might get fed up with him and his whole stupid center." Consider each word of the sentence and how it advances the put-down of Sikes.

4) After four paragraphs of berating artists and an art director, Francis makes a hard turn toward Congress in the fifth paragraph. Is the transition smooth? How does he ease into such a drastic turn?

5) The kicker is a forceful statement expressed in a light, humorous tone. How does Francis provide a wrap-up for the piece?

A conversation with
Samuel Francis

KAREN BROWN: You had no intention originally of going into journalism. How did your route lead you to the profession and *The Washington Times*?

SAMUEL FRANCIS: Well, when I was working on a Ph.D., I got a job in Washington at the Heritage Foundation, and I worked there for about four years. Then I worked in the U.S. Senate for five years as a staff aide. And then I found myself without a job, and I heard there was an opening at *The Washington Times* in the editorial department, and so I applied and was hired.

How would you describe the *Times*?

The Washington Times is a daily newspaper that was founded in 1982. It publishes five days a week. We don't have weekend editions. It's a morning paper.

What about the editorial policy?

Well, it's a conservative editorial page. Ronald Reagan would be the political figure whose policies are most similar to those we support.

Tell me about the paper's readership.

Probably the majority of the readers are in Washington or the immediate suburbs. There is a certain amount of out-of-the-area readers, because we're one of the few major conservative daily newspapers in the country, and we have a lot of conservative people across the country subscribing to the paper.

As you read *The Washington Times* and other papers, do you see the *Times* as significantly different from many other daily papers?

I think that we give more attention to foreign policy, foreign affairs issues, than do a lot of other papers, even large papers. Other than that, except for the ideological cast of the paper, and the editorial page, the Op-Ed section, I don't see any great difference, really.

You said that you're one of the few conservative papers in the nation. Do you see the paper as much more conservative than most dailies?

In terms of editorial policy, yes.

Let's talk about your intentions as you write an editorial. An editorial can persuade, challenge, explain, infuriate. What are some of your general objectives when you write?

Well, my general point in writing an editorial is to communicate an opinion to the reader, to affect the way he or she thinks about the issue being written about, and I try to do it by humor, or by instigating anger or an emotional response, in addition to the factual and logical element of the argument.

Okay, Sam, you've won the ASNE Distinguished Editorial Writing Award two years in a row now, and stand out among editorial writers in the U.S. How do your editorials differ from most others that you see?

I think that if you look at many other editorial pages, you'll see that editorials today tend to be fairly bland. I don't think of them as having much personality. It's a little like cafeteria food. It's institutional writing, really, intended to express the opinions of the institution and the newspaper. What I try to do is to put more personality into editorials than we normally find, not just to express an opinion, but to express a personality behind the opinion.

I know of your interest in history. In preparing for this conversation, I spent some time rereading Pulitzer Prize-winning editorials from the first half of the century, and I noticed how vigorous they were. Your writing seems more in step with those of the past than with most current editorials. What has happened in the industry? Why are so few editorials as expressive as they were in the past?

Well, I think for one thing, the rise of the chains in the newspaper industry has tended to make editorials more bland, so that you get a more oatmeal-like writing, and a desire not to offend anyone. Clearly, if you express a strong opinion you're going to please some people and offend other people.

And I think also the country has become a little more uniform, or homogeneous in its mentality, or at least the newspaper industry has, just for generally intellectual reasons. There's a sort of mainstream consensus, and you don't find too many people in daily newspapers writing outside that consensus, either on the right or on the left.

Does this have anything to do with the issues now? Is it in any way a duller world? Are there fewer issues to get excited about?

I think in the last year or so a great many issues have sort of died. I think communism and defense issues, and things like that, have all but died out. It's very hard to get worried about the Soviet threat or the need for defense spending since 1989. And I think generally we're seeing in the country at large a shift away from old categories, like conservative and liberal, and left and right. That kind of division of opinion will probably cease to be relevant pretty soon.

So where does that leave the editorial writer?

Editorial writers, maybe more than anybody else in the country, are going to have to think up new issues and new things to argue about and form opinions on.

And do you want to suggest some broad areas that editorial writers might consider?

A lot of cultural and social issues are going to remain important. I think issues over race and sexuality and sexual orientation, social issues like that, are going to become increasingly important. You will have continuing debates about the role of government and the role of taxation and public spending. I think people are going to have much less interest in foreign issues and international issues in the future.

You mentioned the intellectual level of those in the industry. What about the intellectual level of the readers? Has that had much of an effect on editorial writing?

There's an assumption among editorial writers that they're smarter than the reader. I don't share that assumption. I think that the reader is likely to be at least as smart as the writer. I don't have much problem with using so-called big words, unusual words, in an editorial. I assume that if readers don't know what it means, they can look it up. Maybe finding a word that they don't know might even pique their interest in the editorial.

In the Washington area, you have a pretty high level of readership, people in the government, people in the military. We have three major universities in the area. I think you can expect a fairly high level of education and intelligence among the readers of editorials in Washington.

Tell me a little bit about the editorials that you read and enjoy besides those in your paper.

I generally don't read too many editorials, to tell

the truth. I read *The Washington Post* editorials, and I read occasionally *The New York Times* editorials, and those in *The Wall Street Journal*. But for the most part, I don't read too many editorials.

Why not?

Well, when I'm reading a newspaper, I'm reading for information, especially if I plan to write on an issue. I really don't want to see other people's opinions. I want to interpret the information for myself.

Okay. How do you get editorial ideas? What's the general process of editorial idea selection at your paper?

As we have organized it in the last year or so, the editorial staff has a meeting at around 2:00 in the afternoon at which the editor of the editorial page, or his deputy, that's me, presides. We go around the room and propose topics to write about. The writers themselves propose the topics, and what their point of view is going to be. And those are either approved or not approved, or sometimes there is an extended discussion. And then usually, the actual writing takes place the next morning, between 9:00 and noon. It's best if you plan the editorial the day before writing it.

Your first editorial here is "Justice reborn." Why did you decide to do this one?

The execution of Ted Bundy had excited a good deal of interest, first of all, because of Bundy's own notoriety, and also because of the celebrations that attended his execution in Florida. I thought this execution called for some comment: generally, the revival of capital punishment, and why people were so happy about Bundy being executed.

A lot of papers had editorials on Ted Bundy's execution. Was this an obligatory editorial, or did you need to say something about the execution?

No. It's not so much an obligatory editorial. I think it was a fairly obvious topic for us because of the publicity around the execution, but also because murder and capital punishment had been so important in the Washington area in the last year because of the murder rate in Washington, because of the issue of punishment in the District and in the presidential campaign. This theme of punishment has been an important theme in our editorials.

Let's go through this one, then. It begins: "When 2,000 volts of lightning slammed into the body of Ted Bundy Tuesday morning, America suddenly became a little bit cleaner and a little bit safer."

In the lead, even in the first line, you use powerful, visual language. You don't say, "When Ted Bundy was executed," but when "lightning slammed into the body." Tell me some of your thoughts in getting those types of nouns and verbs into the lead.

Well, I wanted to make this as graphic as possible and, as you probably noticed, the description of his crimes in one of the later paragraphs is fairly gruesome. But I wanted to emphasize the horror of Bundy's crimes and, at the same time, not to make his own death any less brutal than it was.

There was a good deal of comment in the press about the people who were celebrating his execution, being insensitive to the death of Bundy and generally not understanding what an execution involves. I didn't want to write about his execution and leave myself open to that accusation, that I didn't know what the death of Bundy meant. So the 2,000 volts slamming into his body, and then also later on, the black leather hood in the second column, call attention to the fact that someone is being killed here, and being deliberately killed. Lightning also suggests God striking people with lightning. One theme of the editorial is the justice of retribution.

At the end of that first sentence you said: "America suddenly became a little bit cleaner and a lit-

tle bit safer." You've got a surprise there. I think most people would have expected safer, but not cleaner. What were your thoughts in doing that?

Well, safer because Bundy is a dangerous man, and once he's dead, he's not going to kill anybody else. Cleaner because this is not simply capital punishment to deter, or to protect people, but because it's just. And by killing Bundy, the whole argument here is justice is being reborn, and that makes America cleaner.

That's followed by another series of interesting descriptive words. You refer to three different people, or three different groups. The sentence begins: "But neither the ingenuity of Bundy and his lawyers, the pedantry of judges, nor the lach-rymose quackery of death penalty opponents..." In each case, you use a term that's probably a little less familiar, and that increases in harshness. What was your design there?

By this time, it's probably fairly obvious this editorial was going to defend capital punishment and execution, and "the ingenuity of Bundy and his lawyers" refers to the practice of exploring every legal and public relations maneuver to avoid execution. In other words, I'm alluding here to the arguments that lawyers use to get criminals off, judges will find legal loopholes for them, and death penalty opponents are bleeding-heart sentimentalists.

I don't want to spend a great deal of time making that argument. I just want to more or less dismiss those arguments for the purposes of this editorial, to get on with the larger point here. So I think words like "ingenuity" and "pedantry" and "lachrymose quackery" convey that attitude as concisely as I could imagine.

There is so much compelling writing in the first paragraph. Tell me a little bit about your writing process. Do the right words and phrases come to you the first time around? Do you leave

blanks in the first draft until you find the exact word or phrase you want?

No, they usually come to me the first time around, and I don't know exactly how I can explain that. I think it's an act of creativity, frankly. To me the key of an editorial is the lead sentence, or the lead couple of sentences sometimes.

I find very often if I can get the first sentence, and I think this happened in this case, the editorial flows. I generally find that the kinds of words that I use, and the kinds of expressions that I use, come to me quickly when I'm in the process of writing.

When you start, do you have a general outline, either written or in your mind?

Generally I do, but it's in my mind. I hardly ever have outlines written down. The only time I do that is when I'm writing a research-oriented piece with a lot of different factual aspects to the argument.

Let's talk about the crowd a minute. There are some mixed signals given in your editorial. What was your thinking on the crowd, and how did you want to present them in this editorial?

My personal thought about the crowd is that a lot of what they did was fairly tasteless, that even with Bundy as a notorious killer, his death is still not something you particularly want to be happy about.

But, at the same time, the crowd's reaction was more than just tastelessness. It was also happiness that justice was being done at last. After 10 years and after several murders, finally this man was being executed. There is an ambiguity in the editorial toward this crowd and their reaction. But ultimately, it comes out defending what they did on moral grounds, although it does acknowledge that some of what they did was tasteless.

The second paragraph begins by saying: "The nation's pundits, for the most part, have not yet

weighed in..." Let me ask about timing. Is it important for you to get ahead of what others are going to say, to get in the middle of a debate, to have a last word, or does it matter?

No, in something like this, I don't think it really matters. There are some issues on which we would want to express an opinion before anyone else does, especially if it's a policy issue, a live political issue. But that's not really the case here, and I was not conscious of any need to express an opinion rapidly here.

Later you give some of the details of Bundy's murders. Some of them are pretty gruesome. What are your guidelines about how gory the information can be?

My standing rule is that if it's been published elsewhere, we can talk about it on the editorial page. The reason I went into such grisly detail here about the hacksaw and toothmarks and all of that is that I wanted to emphasize the horror of his crimes, and to contrast that with his own execution. You know, his execution was grim, but it was nothing like what he did to any number of victims. That in itself is pointing toward a defense of capital punishment.

You end very powerfully: "For years many of our leaders have been blind to this truth, and if they now are beginning to grasp it more firmly, that is cause for celebration." You tend to have strong beginnings and strong endings. What things do you want to achieve in the structure of an editorial?

I generally use a structure that's fairly consistent, or at least when I start writing it is. The lead sentence and the lead paragraph are very important to me, to set the tone, and to give the idea of what it's about, and also to point toward the conclusion, or to suggest a conclusion. After the lead, I think of a factual paragraph, maybe two or three paragraphs, if necessary, to lay out the basic facts of the public issue in a more or less objective way, if that's called for. And then, in the third paragraph to set the issue, or to make the first overt statement of opinion, and then the rest of it is the development and the argumentation for that opinion, based on the facts.

The conclusion, in my mind, ought not to summarize, but be an encapsulation to gel the argument. It ought to be fairly short, and it ought to be fairly blunt, and simple. That's the structure of an editorial that I'm comfortable with.

When you start, as you write the lead, do you know what the ending will be?

Almost always, yes. Not in the precise words, but the general idea.

Let's go to the next one, "Bush's uncertain verses." Who wrote the headline?

I did. The *Times*'s editorial writers generally write their own headlines, and these are all mine.

You have some punchy headlines before you even get to the editorial. Tell me a little bit about this editorial, the idea, how it came about.

Well, this is about Salman Rushdie and the threat of Khomeini to kill him for publishing this novel, *The Satanic Verses*. This raised the issue of whether Iranian-inspired terrorism would take place in the United States, directed at bookstores or publishers, or people who bought the book. And after several days President Bush had made a statement on it. The general consensus in our department was that it was not a very strong statement, given the serious threat that this kind of terrorism was inspiring and what it might mean for the future, not just for Rushdie himself, but for a lot of other people involved. And so this is really the genesis of this editorial.

In the second paragraph, you mention "the Western world's literati," and you also refer to them as "savants." Is it important in an editorial to clearly draw the good guys and the bad guys?

Very often it is. There are some characters in an editorial who may have to be in there, and it's not really important to characterize them in that way, but I think that very, very often, you do want to make a clear distinction between good guys and bad guys.

In this one, I think you end up with four groups or individuals. You have Rushdie, and the ayatollah and his government, then the intellectuals, and Bush and his government. Can you clearly say who are the good guys and the bad guys?

Well, I think it's clear in the editorial that the ayatollah and his people are not good guys. Rushdie is not a bad guy, but he's not really a good guy. He's not a helpless martyr or an innocent victim here so much. I think the idea is that Rushdie has gone to ground in the bunkers, and that raises a question about Rushdie here. The editorial is not going to be a pure defense of Rushdie as against Khomeini. It's going to be something else. The stuff about the literati strapping on sword and buckler, that's intended as a put-down of the literati, obviously. But they're not really bad people either. It's just that you don't expect much more from them.

But then in the third paragraph, the focus shifts. This piece is not going to be about Rushdie, or the intellectuals, but instead, it's about the president and his lack of clarity on the issue. I think this is your "nut graph," the paragraph in which you set the issue. Would you agree?

Yes.

It's also a very visual paragraph, in that you say that "12 European states have defiantly slapped," and that "President Bush and Secretary of State

James Baker have merely stuck out their tongues." Most writers would have used some diplomatic terms. Do you have to resist that?

It depends on the mood I'm in. I have an academic background, and my natural inclination is to use that kind of diplomatic or formal language. But writing editorials has helped to break me of that habit, which I think is good. In editorials you want graphic expression and visual images, not all the time, maybe, but certainly at key points in an editorial, I think those are called for. I would look for certain key points in the editorials that need what Don Fry has called a "gold coin." You don't want gold coins all the way through the editorial, but you want to find certain turning points, certain points in the argument you're trying to make. By making those points highly graphic and visual, I think you can make them stick in the reader's mind.

The first sentence of this paragraph, "Intellectuals, of course, cannot be expected to offer a more strenuous response to the ayatollah's terrorism than the gestures from which they make their living," is a fairly academic, formal sentence, I think. But the concluding sentence of the paragraph, where you want to make the point, is what you want to be graphic here.

Yes, but actually you've set up the intellectuals so well in the previous paragraph with the reference to "gunsights on a member of the international literary brotherhood," which caused "the savants [to] begin to sweat." After that the next sentence doesn't come off as dry and academic, because you still have the humor from the previous reference, the sneer at intellectuals in the previous sentence.

About the fourth paragraph you proceed in a rather straightforward way, developing the argument without the use of catchy phrases or images. You discuss what the president's done and what he should do. Yet the writing is still clear and crisp, interesting and compelling. What

**keeps it compelling, even though you're not us-
ing a lot of graphic writing along the way?**

At that point we've had enough of the rhetorical
froth, and we need to get down to the factual basis
of this, the claims that I have been making. What
exactly has Bush said and done about terrorism,
and how true are those statements? What exactly
are they going to do to protect the United States or
other people from this maniac? By making those
sorts of undecorated factual exercises there, that's
the cake on the icing that's in the first part.

I know writers, I'm sure you do too, especially
young writers who want to get through with just
the icing, the colorful language. That doesn't work.
I don't think it works much better if you just have
the cake, the straight facts, with no icing, which is
what most editorials today tend to be.

Right.

Sometimes you don't get cake or icing. [Laughter]

**That's a pretty good analogy. Since I haven't
eaten much today, let me move on. The editorial
continues with a series of very strong sentences
about the president and his administration's
policies on terrorism. Then you end by returning to the lead, Mr. Rushdie and the "eggheads."
Why is it important to return to the lead in the
kicker?**

Well, I think whenever you have an editorial that
has a strong lead, or an involved lead like this one
does, it's important to return to it to frame the editorial. In doing that, in returning to it, you answer a
logical question that may be in the reader's mind:
What does this beginning have to do with anything?

I'm saying here in the lead, actually in the first
two paragraphs, that intellectuals are upset about
what Khomeini has done, but they're not doing
very much about it. Governments ought to do more,
but it's our opinion that our government may not be

doing much of anything. Maybe Mr. Bush is no
more of a strong leader on this than are the intellectuals. That's what the conclusion is intended to suggest.

**Do you recall how much time you spent in doing
the whole editorial?**

I would say an hour, hour and a half, maybe.

**Let's look at "Hypocrisy on the right?" You're
taking the unpopular point of view with conservatives here. What made you decide to do this?**

Well, last summer *The Washington Times* came up
with a number of stories on sex scandals in Washington. We'd had several stories, sort of spin-offs
of these, about the sex scandals involving various
liberals and Democrats. Jim Wright had resigned.
The Crommelin case was basically broken by our
paper in the spring. The John Mack story, about
the Jim Wright aide, had also been broken, not by
our paper, but in the same time period. And there
was a good deal of exulting, and I thought self-
congratulation, among many conservatives about
corruption among liberals.
    My response to this was that there was a tenden-
cy among conservatives to be a little smug about it,
and if you look at the record carefully, you can see
that they didn't have that much to boast about
themselves. I just wanted to poke a hole in some of
their smugness, basically.

Burst some balloons.

Yes.

**What about the reader? How much consistency
should a reader expect in the editorials?**

I think for a page that has a high ideological identity, like ours or various liberal newspapers, consistency is very important if it's going to be re-

garded as an honest page. I think without that attention to consistency, you're going to get a reputation for simple partisanism.

What I'm saying is, you can be ideologically intense, and serious, without being partisan. Having an ideological identity is to take a philosophy and present it as a guide to life, to politics, to behavior, and to public issues. By being partisan, I mean simply supporting members of one party, or one side of the aisle, over another.

If you take the ideological identity, you don't necessarily have to be partisan, because you can say that either side of the aisle has violated, or been unfaithful to, that ideological identity, depending on the circumstances.

So then, is there an advantage, when these opportunities arise, in which you can be consistent with the philosophy, but not be partisan?

Yes.

There's another interesting aspect to this. Not only were you writing an editorial that tended to go against what many would expect from your paper, but you also touched on personal connections for yourself and the paper. For one thing, Crommelin worked for John East, as you had. Did you know him?

Yes. He was my supervisor for nine months. I knew the circumstances of the incident that he was involved in, but this editorial was not written until after he had pled guilty and had been sentenced. Also the editorial is not centered on Crommelin so much as it is on the conservative community. So I really don't think there was any kind of conflict of interest there.

In the editorial you mentioned that a *Washington Times* editor had been involved in one of the scandals. What are the rules when you're writing about, or dealing with, issues or people with

whom you have connections?

I'm not aware of any such guidelines at the newspaper. As you know, I worked in the Senate for
several years. I've been in Washington for several
years. There have been incidents in which I have
not written on subjects because of personal feelings, or personalities involved in issues, and so
I'm alive to this consideration.

I don't think, in our department, it comes up that
much, to tell the truth. I felt that it was necessary,
for the editorial, to put that reference to the editor
in. I had not actually thought about that when I
started writing the thing. I started to talk about
Lukens, Crommelin, and Jim Bakker. But then as I
was writing it, it suddenly occurred to me that one
of our own editors had also resigned over an incident, and we had mentioned that. In fact, we had
broken that story by mentioning it in one of our
pieces on the scandals.

It just struck me that it would be woefully dis-
honest if I didn't note that in this piece. And I
thought, in fact, it would strengthen the piece if I
did mention it.

**On other matters, you wrote of Jim Bakker. Did
you have any thoughts about the propriety of using "thumping mattresses" to describe sexual
activity?**

[Laughs] No. Well, I mean, I wondered at the time
whether this would actually get through or not. But
all I can say is we live in an age when a leading
congressman can talk about his homosexual liaison
with prostitutes and remain in office, and it seems
to me that, by today's standards, "thumping mattresses" is not at all an improper usage here, given
the kind of things that are daily fare in the newspapers and television and movies and everywhere
else. Of course, "thumping mattresses" is sort of a
roundabout way of talking about the sexual en-
counters there.

You weren't sure if it would get through. Who does it go through? Just the copy desk?

It goes past the editor of the page, past the editor of the newspaper, and past the copy desk. I don't think either Tony Snow, editorial page editor, or Arnaud de Borchgrave, the editor of the newspaper, would have any problem with it. There have been questions of propriety raised by the copy desk, though not in this case, as far as I know. When I'm editing editorials, I not infrequently take out things by other writers that I think are improper or transgress the standards, usually sexual in nature.

Okay. Let's go to "Rapping garbage as 'art.'" This was based on information from an article in your paper, right?

Yeah.

About what percentage of your editorials are drawn from stories in the paper?

I would say 80, 90 percent are. I would say almost all of them are.

Why did you decide to do this one?

This actually grew out of kind of a controversy in the editorial department. One of our writers originally wanted to do a piece on rap music based on David Mills's article in our paper, and he wanted his pitch to be that rap music inspires violence and condones drugs, and that it ought to be controlled by the police.

Our editor, I think, and I took the view that this was really a heavy-handed approach, and that we ought to take a lighter approach. If you take the heavy approach, you're going to wind up with a situation like you did in the '50s when people wanted to outlaw Elvis Presley and block out his movements below the hips, and that sort of thing, and you would generally make fools of yourselves.

The approach I've tried to take here was a somewhat different one, that there's something missing in rap music, or at least this version of it.

I'm going to take a leap of faith here and assume that the topic of rap music is a subject on which you would have less background information than on most subjects that you write about.

Uh-huh.

How much information is it necessary for you to know to do a good editorial? Were you comfortable doing this one?

I was fairly comfortable, because the Mills story was a fairly thorough story, and the Mills story also sort of bounced off of issues that had been floating around in the Washington community for a while.

I raise the question because some experts on rap music, my son and some other teen-agers I know for instance, would say that the people mentioned here in the lyrics are not typical of rap music.

That may be. I think that's probably true, but it's a certain kind of rap music that I'm talking about here. I'm talking about a specific group and a specific song, and specific individuals. I think that's really what it's centered on.

A train of thought throughout the editorial suggests that the argument is not just about rap music, but it is the larger question of what is art. How much of the editorial is about rap music, and how much is really about art and what purposes it serves?

Well, I think it really is about art, and this connects with the whole Mapplethorpe issue, and the National Endowment of the Arts issue that was debated throughout the year. In all of these cases, there's a tendency for the defenders to say, "Well, this is realistic," or, "This kind of behavior really happens, and therefore, to portray it is being realistic."

I'm basically trying to clarify a distinction about the relationship between art and reality here. I'm saying that art never disguises reality, but it doesn't surrender to it, either. It tries maybe to rise above it.

Even in the second paragraph, you say: "The real question about rap, especially the hard-core variety, is whether it says anything worth listening to."

In the last paragraph, you wrote: "No one will much care about the 'inner me' of Schooly D and his buddies if all that's inside them is the ugliness they brag about and all that comes out is the artistic equivalent of diarrhea." In the particularly sensitive racial climate of Washington, and when much of rap music has come from a young society that feels that nobody cares, did that closing statement present any problems of sensitivity for you?

Well, it does not for me because I'm talking about Schooly D and his particular group as specific individuals, and it seems to me that the racial sensitivity here really ought to be focused on him and his friends, not on the editorial, because they're the ones who are missing the reality of urban life, actually.

That's the reality that you mention in the fifth paragraph: "...family members working for each other, students trying to elevate themselves, community leaders risking their lives to control the garbage rappers celebrate."

Yes.

How important is it to have editorials that address changes in society rather than just major political issues?

I think that's a primary role for editorials. A news-paper or an editorial page ought to be read by the entire community, not just by people who are in-terested in politics or public issues, but any public event, whether it's a cultural event, or political, or a sports event, religion, morality, family life, any-thing like that, I think ought to be a possible sub-ject for an editorial. To do that strengthens an edi-torial page. It broadens the appeal, and it allows for a broader vision for the newspaper.

I mentioned ideological identity earlier, but I think the test of any set of beliefs is its application to human life, to the reality of human life, and if it can only be applied in politics, or a very narrow band of human life, then it's probably not worth very much. But I think if you can have a consistent ideological or philosophical vision on an editorial page about many aspects of life, that strengthens the newspaper, and what you're trying to say.

Let's go to the last one then, and that's "Urine the money." Again, your headline stands out.

I really wondered if this head was going to go through. [Laughter]

You didn't get any questions about it?

I don't think I did, no.

This one was a little less than a month after the last one, which was about art.

Yes. It was part of a number of editorials on this theme that we ran for several months, actually.

In this one, you introduced the situation and provided an emphatic ending to the first para-graph by noting that some questionable art is paid for by "you and your tax dollars." I think that's one of the few times you use the second person in addressing the reader. Why did you decide to do it there?

Well, whenever you're talking about something that involves public money and tax dollars, it may strengthen the argument, or the appeal, to personalize it with the second person. I frequently do that, actually; whenever I talk about tax dollars in the context of something I'm against, I'll use the second person.

That's a situation in which many would say it's paid for by government funds.
The structure of this piece is particularly interesting because it builds, and the major point is at the end. It starts with "Cactus Jack" being a heel, and moves on to Jason Sikes, and then takes a turn. You realize by about the fifth paragraph that it's not just these two, but the Congress is composed of some heels. Then you state the main point rather forcefully in the last paragraph. What were your intentions in using that structure?

Well, unlike the execution of Ted Bundy, or some of the other things I was writing about, this was not a well-known story. This was based on a story, I think it was exclusive in our paper, about this Cactus Jack and the Phoenix art museum, and I felt that a good bit of detail about exactly what had happened, and what he did and what was said, was important to making the point. In fact, the factual buildup here is almost the entire editorial.

But I also wanted to draw the parallel here between the artists who are freeloading off of the taxpayer and the congressmen who are freeloading in the sense that they don't want any criticism. So basically, you have two villains here, as people who are exploiting or using their position for unfair advantages.

And the good guy is present in a little quieter sense, and that's the taxpayer?

Yes.

I started this conversation by noting that you hadn't planned to be a journalist. Your education and experiences were in other areas. As an outsider coming in, do you avoid much of what could be considered traditional journalistic writing?

Well, I think I probably do and I don't. I don't have any idea how to do traditional journalistic writing. I just write naturally. I write things that I think will convey information and ideas, and I do it in a way that will be understandable and entertaining to the reader.

Linnet Myers
Government Reporting

LINNET MYERS grew up in Chicago on the South Side. She attended the University of Oregon, the University of Chicago, Antioch College, and Columbia College in Chicago before graduating from Barnard in 1978. She majored in history and worked for the *Columbia Spectator,* the university's daily paper. She started at the *Register*, a weekly on Cape Cod. In 1979, she joined *The Hartford Courant* as a courts and government reporter. She won a fellowship with the Inter-American Press Association for an exchange program in Caracas, Venezuela. In 1983, she joined the *Chicago Tribune* as a general assignment reporter, moving eventually to the criminal court beat. After two and a half years, she moved to features, where she wrote these prize-winning stories.

Humanity on trial

FEBRUARY 12, 1989

Murderers walk these halls, and the mothers of murderers, and the mothers of the murdered too.

This is 26th and California.

Step through the metal detectors and enter the multicolored stream of humanity that flows through the Criminal Court building each day. It is the largest felony-trial system under one roof in the United States. In 34 courtrooms, nothing but felonies are heard: murders, manslaughters, sexual assaults, armed robberies, burglaries, drug cases. Last year, 19,632 cases were heard here.

Officially, it is the Cook County Circuit Court, Criminal Division. But those who work here refer to it by its near Southwest Side location, 26th Street and California Boulevard—known simply as "26th & Cal."

Outside, on the building's noble limestone walls, are carved the Latin words *Veritas* and *Justitia*—truth and justice.

Inside is a world the average Chicagoan never sees.

Walk down the hallway to the lobby of the building's old section, opened by Anton Cermak on April Fool's Day, 1929. With its imposing columns and ornate ceiling, this was the main lobby when, despite Prohibition and the St. Valentine's Day Massacre of that year, crime wasn't as rampant as it is today and there were only 15 courtrooms here.

The 19 new courtrooms and judges—added in 1978—cut the caseloads from a high of about 350 per judge, said Richard J. Fitzgerald, who was the building's chief judge until he resigned last month. "And that's what the judges have now," he said. "It's right back where we were."

From the lobby, take the elevator to the fourth floor, Courtroom 402. This is Violence Court, and only the worst cases—homicides and sex crimes—qualify.

Violence Court is the first stop for suspects who have just been arrested. There are no full trials here. Cases are quickly read and bonds are set during hearings that last only a few minutes each.

This courtroom gives a taste of an overwhelming fact: crime in Chicago. Observers here watch criminal after criminal come and go as if in some grisly surrealistic play.

Take a seat and watch as defendants are led in from the lockup, one by one. The deputies first bring in Nisi Nunzio, charged with sexually fondling a little girl at the Shedd Aquarium. "It was a setup," Nunzio begins.

"What's that?" asks Judge Michael Bolan, looking up from his papers. "Oh, it's a setup, okay."

The judge hears the evidence from Richard Stevens, an assistant state's attorney. "The 10-year-old victim, who was watching the fish, felt the defendant behind her," Stevens says.

Stevens reads the defendant's background: He has convictions for contributing to the delinquency of a minor and for public indecency. Security guards at the aquarium had noticed him there before, acting suspiciously, Stevens says.

Judge Bolan sets the bond at $10,000 and adds a condition: Nunzio can't return to the aquarium while the case is pending. "You're off aquarium duty," the judge says. "Do you understand?"

Nunzio is led away, and Antonio Balderos is led in. Prosecutor John Mahoney reads the charges: murder, armed robbery, burglary, theft.

"That's a mouthful," says the judge. It is a potential death-penalty case; Balderos is ordered held without bond and is led away.

Next, Reginald Morgan, charged with sexual assault. Defense lawyer Thomas Breen objects because Morgan has been indicted by a grand jury without a preliminary hearing, at which the defense could present its case. The objection is routine, but today Breen decides to add a little emphasis. "We're shocked," Breen says.

"For the record, he's shocked," says the judge.

On some days, things are almost sedate at Violence Court. On others, 12 or 13 murder cases are heard in a single afternoon. Still others bring obscene parades of child molesters, rapists, or young gang members charged with killing one another over nothing.

It is here that you hear of the crimes that don't make the news—the everyday murders, run-of-the-mill, the ones reporters call "cheap." In a saner place, they would be news—in some places, even big news. But not here. Here murder has somehow become part of everyday life.

There were 660 homicides in Chicago last year. In Violence Court, that statistic becomes real.

There are robbery murders, gang murders, domestic murders, insanity murders, arson murders, tavern-fight murders, child-abuse murders, contract murders, and rape murders.

There also are murders over things like a piece of banana pie, a girlfriend who turned out to be a boyfriend, or a feud about something nobody can remember—things that can almost seem funny, here in this strange and violent world.

One day a man named Andre Collins was brought in after being picked up on a warrant for an armed-robbery murder. The paperwork was in duplicate; Judge Bolan announced that Collins was charged with two murders.

Collins didn't react at all when the first charge was read, but he wasn't ready to accept two. "Uh-uh," he objected. "Wasn't no two." Spectators giggled, and Judge Bolan turned his chair around, broke into laughter, and turned back again a moment later, his face red.

"Sometimes you have to turn your chair to the wall so you don't laugh out loud," Bolan said in a recent interview. "Or I bite my hand because I don't want to lose my decorum. There's only one judge in the room, and if you lose it, the whole place loses it."

Yet there is a chill to the humor, and Judge Bolan sometimes wonders what he is accomplishing.

"It's frustrating, you know, that tomorrow there's going to be a whole new batch," he said. "It's of a continuing nature. You'd like to see some kind of reward, and there's no clear lines here of any reward. I don't build any buildings, I don't invent computer chips. Is the world any better for what I'm doing here? I ask myself, 'What are you doing, Michael?'

"You can get totally immersed in this building.... There's a Criminal Court personality: You become cynical as hell, nothing is taken at face value, you cross-examine everything. Nobody's innocent. Innocence is something that's lost in childhood.

"But when a person is accused of a bad act, that doesn't sum up that person. I still believe very much in the innate worth of all human beings. If you ever lose that, you ought to hang it up. Even if they've done a bad thing, that's a human being suffering there.... And the victims too are suffering. They're hurt. They're all hurt people."

Bolan finds that people always ask about his job.

"No matter who they are, they still want to know what's happening at the slime pit, at 26th Street, at slice-of-life land," he said. "It's human nature with all its pretenses stripped away.... Headquarters for tales from the dark side."

Along with the judge, the regular cast in Violence Court includes defense lawyers, a team of prosecutors, and various police officers, who wait in the front rows for their cases to be called.

Sitting in the otherwise empty jury box are the news reporters, paid observers of this uncommon parade. As the weeks go by, a young city news bureau reporter watches each day in growing disgust.

"What is *wrong* with these people?" she whispers to another reporter. "What is *wrong* with them? What is going on here?"

As another lively day comes to an end, an assistant public defender leans over and whispers to those near him, "Every defendant is a jewel in the crown of life."

Violence Court is only the beginning. From here, the defendants are arraigned and then prepare to go to trial.

* * *

Murder trials are heard every week in the Criminal Court; often several are going on at once in the building's various trial courtrooms. Watch for a while and you'll begin to understand the lawyers' jargon, the legal motions, the judges who get angry if you talk.

To begin, open the heavy wooden door to a sixth-floor courtroom and watch defendant Johnny Freeman on the witness stand.

He is testifying about the day 200 people surrounded him outside a Henry Horner Homes public housing building and angrily accused him of raping and killing a 5-year-old girl.

"Two boys jumped in front of me with baseball bats," Freeman is saying. "I started to run.... The whole crowd came at me."

Police saved Freeman from the crowd that day; they saved him for a Criminal Court trial.

Prosecutor William Hibbler now tells the jury that Freeman pushed Shavanna McCann from a 13th-floor window as the child clung to the ledge screaming, "Mama! Mama!"

"Shavanna McCann is still crying out," Hibbler says. "Not for Mama, but for justice."

Freeman got life in prison without parole. He was three months short of his 18th birthday when he committed the crime, three months too young for the death penalty.

Open another courtroom door on another day in another month.

Listen as the written confession of gang member Daniel Pena is read. "It was like—how you say—a payback," his confession says. "They kill one of ours; we kill one of theirs."

Stay in the Criminal Court awhile, and all gang-war murders start to sound alike. In another one, a friend of gang member Luis "Popeye" Toledo explains why Popeye died in a gang battle:

"I used to tell him it's stupid," she says. "It's all us Latinos killing each other.... Our own race is killing itself, and that sounds sad. It's really sad.

"But he said, 'If it's got to be, it's got to be.'... He

had it in his heart."

In yet another gang case, Lawrence Taylor fired at a rival gang member and instead hit Laketa Crosby, 9, a girl jumping rope in front of the Cabrini-Green public housing complex.

Taylor rushed over and cradled her in his arms. "Please, Keta, don't die," he said. "I'll do anything...if she lives. I'll take care of her." Keta died, and Taylor got 80 years.

* * *

Lorenzo Molina is accused of murdering Humberto Sotelo, the man who allegedly killed Molina's father 15 years ago in a tiny Mexican town. It was the most recent killing in a decades-old feud, say police detectives Tony Jin and William Baldree.

The detectives say Molina doesn't know what started the feud; neither do other family members. "They usually start over something simple," Jin tells you. "We asked them, 'Did somebody steal a chicken or call someone's daughter a whore?' They said, 'We don't know.'"

Michele Schwartz sits on the witness stand, her arms outstretched, demonstrating how she shot her husband, the Rev. Charles Jones. The couple, both missionaries, had been arguing over who saved more souls.

Schwartz says she fired in self-defense and is acquitted. "I'm just a servant of the Lord," she tells you as she leaves the courtroom.

Mack Lewis was convicted of killing his girlfriend's father, Clarence Marshall, after Marshall failed to share some banana pudding pie on Easter Sunday. "He was saying how good the pie was and didn't bring any home," a prosecutor says.

Loveless Austin's girlfriend turned out to be a man. During an intimate moment, he discovered that "Stella Essie" was actually Jerome Brent. The next day, Austin came back with a sledgehammer and a knife, seeking revenge. He got 40 years in prison.

Lon Shultz, an assistant state's attorney, later tells you that Austin got the name "Loveless" because "his father insisted on him being named that."

* * *

The little girl standing outside a second-floor courtroom looks confused, her face twisted into a frown, as if trying to remember something.

During the trial she just attended, she noticed that someone "said my mama's name." The child, Leslie Morris, was 14 months old when a man named D'arthagan Sargent murdered her mother. Now she is 6.

Police arrived at the scene to find tiny bloody handprints on the refrigerator and little footprints of blood leading across the floor. "The girl is incredible," her father tells you. "She managed to open the refrigerator and eat the raw bacon and cake that was on the bottom shelf." She was found after two days, cuddled against her dead mother.

"The mind is a wonderful thing," says her father, Raymond Morris. "She doesn't remember that night."

Or does she? For years, no one could sleep in front of Leslie. "When you went to sleep, she'd raise your eyelids," says her aunt. Her father says she'd follow him everywhere, so closely underfoot that "I've stepped on her." She'd wake from nightmares, "hollering, crying, shaking," he says.

"Leslie doesn't know what it is. But we know."

The child's mother, Rhonda Barnes, was strangled by Sargent, an ex-convict who had committed six rapes by the age of 15, says Linda Woloshin, an assistant state's attorney. Sargent served five years for those crimes and then was released.

"Psychiatrists were pleased with his conduct," Woloshin tells you. "Eight days after his release, he raped again." He served eight years that time and again was freed. Two years after that, he murdered Leslie's mother.

As the prosecutor talks, the child is still frowning in that peculiar way. You wonder if she understands. Or if anyone does.

* * *

You've heard there's a murder trial going on in the courtroom of Judge Thomas Maloney. On your way there, you see a man and woman talking in the hallway. Suddenly the woman faints, falling flat, so that her face hits the floor.

You hurry over, touch her gently, and she opens her eyes. "I tried so hard," she tells you, still dazed. "I'm so tired. I'm so tired.... I got to be with my child."

The man she was talking to, Assistant Public Defender Michael King, feels terrible. He didn't know she'd take it so hard. The woman is the mother of the man on trial, who is accused of murdering his wife. She is also the one who discovered the body and was preparing to be a witness. She fainted when King showed her pictures of the corpse.

"It's got to be a dream," she is saying as the paramedics arrive. "It's got to be a dream."

* * *

With time, you begin to learn the rules of the Criminal Court. Some are rules of law and evidence. Others are unwritten rules.

There's the Criminal Court rule of motherhood: Mothers will lie for their children. A mother will swear to tell the truth and then testify that her son was with her, when he was in fact committing murder.

A mother will stand up for her son—unless he was a baby and was beaten to death by her husband or boyfriend. Then it is likely that the mother will be loyal to her lover, not to her dead son.

There are rules that say it's hard to get a murder conviction for a child-abuse killing, because the grown-ups often say they were "disciplining" the children and didn't mean to kill.

There are rules that say little children who are sexually assaulted better be old enough not only to say what happened but also to know what day it is, what time it is, what truth is, what a lie is. Because they have to prove they're "competent" before they can even testify.

Other rules say the rape of a woman deserves the same punishment as the sale of 15 grams of cocaine. Rules say a rapist can get out of prison and rape again—and again—before he is put away for good.

There's a rule that says a 40-year prison term is really a 20-year term and a 10-year sentence really means 5 because of the prison system of "day-for-day time off."

Rules say you may commit the same crime as someone else but your sentence may vary greatly, depending on which judge you have. Also, all judges here are officially competent, but some are never assigned "heater" cases—the big cases that make the news.

Rules say the murder of a "dirty victim"—like a gang member or a vagrant—isn't good, but it's not as bad as the murder of a "clean victim." Rules say there's no sexism, but it's easier to get off if you're a woman.

Rules say there's no racism, but if you want to escape the death penalty, statistics indicate it's probably better to murder a black person than a white person.

As the weeks and months pass, you find yourself getting used to murder. You no longer flinch at the bloody pictures; the details become facts instead of horror stories. Then you walk in on a child-abuse murder trial.

"This is a photo of the belt you used to strike Keith, isn't it?" asks Assistant State's Attorney Tom Gibbons, who is cross-examining defendant Edward Thirston.

"Looks like it," answers Thirston, who is on trial for murdering 22-month-old Keith Jones.

"Is that where you struck the baby with the belt?"

"No," the defendant says.

Why, then, were welts on the dead baby's back, legs, arms, buttocks, and stomach?

"I don't know," says Thirston.

"It's a mystery?"

"To me it's a mystery."

* * *

The families of the dead sit in rows in the courtrooms. They're here for justice.

As you watch the trials, you watch them too. The cases can be dramatic, intriguing, absorbing. But when you glance over at the families, you remember how real they are. And how horrible.

"It's not TV," Assistant State's Attorney George Ellison tells a jury during the trial of Michael Bryant, charged with a brutal rape and murder. "It's real life, and it is horrid and it is atrocious."

The pain is etched on the faces of those whose loved ones were killed. You see where most of them are from: They're poor, they're black or Hispanic. They live in the ghetto, and maybe they should be used to violence. They're not. Their pain is so real you could reach out and grab it. Their eyes haunt you.

You meet a young man in the hallway. You know you've seen him before—you recognize the anguish in his dark eyes. Then you realize: His mother was killed in an arson fire, and you watched the arsonist's trial.

You start to wonder: How many deaths have you heard about? How many killers have you seen? Day by day, the anger around you seems to build. Sometimes the horror slams down like a sledgehammer. The judges and lawyers try to fit it all neatly into the courtrooms, the proceedings, the scientific evidence. It doesn't fit.

A weeping mother runs from a courtroom. The crime-lab microanalyst on the witness stand is using technical terms, but that can't sterilize the bloodstains on her murdered daughter's clothes.

The who, what, when, and where of each case have been answered. Only the why remains.

Observations and questions

1) Linnet Myers writes large parts of this series in the second person, beginning with the third paragraph: "[You] Step through the metal detectors..." Myers gains immediacy, but presents the readers with a form they don't expect in newspapers. Is this tradeoff worth it?

2) Throughout the series, Myers uses imagery of drama, e.g., "Observers here watch criminal after criminal come and go as if in some grisly surrealistic play." Study how she uses this image as a unifying device without becoming artsy.

3) Even in pieces as long as these, readers may have trouble dealing with so many characters. Study how Myers clusters named characters, separates them, differentiates them, details some and smudges others, and chooses carefully who speaks and who does not. Notice the lack of traditional identifiers, such as age, address, etc.

4) Occasionally, Myers editorializes in her word choices, as in this passage: "On some days, things are almost sedate at Violence Court. On others, 12 or 13 murder cases are heard in a single afternoon. Still others bring *obscene* parades of child molesters, rapists, or young gang members charged with killing one another *over nothing*." Are feature writers free to editorialize, even lightly? Do some subjects call out for opinion?

5) As a Chicago reporter, Myers uses the mythology of her city: "It is here that you hear of the crimes that don't make the news—the everyday murders, run-of-the-mill, the ones reporters call 'cheap.' In a saner place, they would be news—in some places, even big news. But not here. Here murder has somehow become part of everyday life." Study how she makes her readers aware of the emotional and social cost of Chicago's pride in its tough-guy image.

6) Judge Bolan says, "No matter who they are, they still

want to know what's happening at the slime pit, at 26th Street, at slice-of-life land....It's human nature with all its pretenses stripped away....Headquarters for tales from the dark side." Consider this passage as a potential kicker, especially the way it would determine what the reader takes away from this story.

7) As much as we might admire Myers's wonderful "rules" section, we have to ask if readers might miss the irony and take it straight. How could we frame this part to keep readers from going astray?

8) Notice how the imagery of mothers appears at the beginning and end of this piece. What effects do tying the lead and ending have for readers, both in general and in this story?

Born losers

FEBRUARY 13, 1989

In the world of the Criminal Court, where murder is common and armed robbery routine, some crimes stand out.

The victims are chosen at random. The violence is incredible, yet there was no money to gain, no particular anger to vent, no revenge to seek.

The facts of the cases are stated in the courtrooms: what the defendants did, when, where, to whom. Yet questions are left in the minds of those watching the trials: Why did they do it? How could anyone do it?

The defendants usually sit silently through their trials, revealing little. It is only after further investigation, whose results are sometimes presented at sentencing hearings, that the roots of their violence show.

* * *

John Spires entered the juvenile justice system in 1964, a victim of child abuse. He graduated a violent criminal, class of '76.

Spires now is serving a 120-year prison sentence. He raped children.

When he was a child himself, 7 years old, John Spires slit his wrists in a suicide attempt and was admitted to Chicago State Hospital, say psychiatric records. It was the first of many suicide attempts and psychiatric hospitalizations.

When he was 9, Spires ran away from home with his 11-year-old sister. On July 8, 1964, Chicago's *American* ran a story about it that called the children "young vagabonds" and said they "had spent their days in Riverview Amusement Park, had slept in hallways, had stolen a woman's purse and picked a man's wallet, and had a steady diet of hot dogs and hamburgers."

It didn't tell of how their parents had beaten them or how they had been chained to their beds. Or of the times they were yanked from their sleep by their father—a violent alcoholic—or locked in closets by their mother or sexually abused by their uncle.

Child abuse, in those days, wasn't a public issue.

The brief item did say that John and Jean were taken to the Audy home for juvenile delinquents. But there was no follow-up story about how Spires, at age 9, was sexually assaulted by the older, tougher boys there.

Many times the police picked up John and Jean, sometimes with their younger sister, Marie, who said she first ran away with them when she was about 6.

"We would sleep on roofs," said Marie (both sisters asked that their real names not be used). "One time we slept in a hot dog stand and one time—the scariest time—was when we slept in a hole in the ground where they were doing construction."

John Spires seemed to be his parents' favorite target, his sisters said. "The kid could do no right," Jean said, "no matter what he did."

Spires's first crime was theft. His crimes became violent when he turned 21.

It was then that Spires committed two rapes: one of an 11-year-old girl, the other of a 16-year-old. He was convicted, served three years in prison, and was released, more violent than ever.

Within a year and a half, he committed four more rapes: all of schoolgirls aged 12 or 13. Before police suspected him, Spires went to a psychiatrist named Andrew Pundy, "asking for brain surgery in order to stop his compulsion to rape," according to a psychiatric report.

Spires told the psychiatrist that he was haunted by fantasies of rape. "I was obsessed," Spires said in an interview at Menard Prison, where he is serving his term.

Spires asked for a lobotomy. Pundy didn't agree but began to treat him. At the same time, Spires asked his family members to watch him—to make sure he didn't leave the house alone.

As time passed, police began to suspect that Spires had committed the rapes. He was eventually arrested and convicted of four counts of aggravated criminal sexual assault. In Courtroom 506 of the Criminal Court, Spires watched as the girls testified against him.

"I wanted to try to make them feel better, let them know it wasn't them, that it wasn't their fault, that I was sorry," he said. "But I couldn't. I listened to them. I thought, 'Is that really me they're talking about?'... I really wanted to get under the table and just hide."

Today, Spires is a soft-spoken young man who talks with a bland melancholy about regrets that came far too late. "I feel like an animal," he said. "I feel like I should be taken out in the morning and shot."

To Jean and Marie, their brother John is more sick than criminal. Both women said they went through long-term therapy themselves to overcome the psychological damage done during their childhoods.

Jean was agoraphobic; for a year, she wouldn't leave her home, fearful of the outside world. Marie suffered anxiety attacks, rushing to hospital emergency rooms when her breath got short and her heart pounded so wildly that she thought she would die. There was nothing physically wrong with her; it was old fears from the abuse, coming back.

"I have a daughter, and if someone raped her, I would want to kill him," Jean said. "But John is my brother. And I feel if he had gotten help when he was younger, maybe he wouldn't do the things he's done."

While his victims testified in court, Spires wondered what he had done to their lives.

"I remember things that happened in my past and I know what it did to me and prayed I didn't (do the same thing to them)," he said. "I hope they have their lives together, working and in a relationship—a loving relationship—that I didn't mess anything like that up for them. A lot of times I've wondered how they're doing. I thought of writing them a letter, but every time I brought it up, someone said, 'Are you crazy?'... It'd probably scare them just to hear from me. They probably wish I was dead."

Judge Thomas Hett gave Spires a 240-year prison term, which was later reduced to 120 years. Spires, 33, could be released after serving 60 years, if he lives that long.

Spires first was sent to Stateville Prison. The picture on his prisoner identification card shows him with two black eyes; his fellow prisoners also hate the crime of child rape.

"In Stateville, I got jumped, in fights all the time because of the crime itself," Spires said. "I figure it was all part of the punishment. It's probably the worst thing you can do. I'd rather be here for murder."

Now, in the relative calm of Menard Prison's psychiatric unit, Spires is no longer the victim of other inmates' violence.

"I'm comfortable in here," he said, "because I know I can't hurt nobody."

* * *

Society made its feelings known during a Criminal Court sentencing hearing when Spires was ordered to prison, virtually for life.

A sentencing hearing, held after a defendant has been found guilty of a crime, is generally the last procedure a defendant goes through at the Criminal Court building at 26th Street and California Boulevard. His fate—probation, a prison term, or a death sentence—is decided at this stage.

A judge or jury must consider the defendant's background before deciding on the punishment, so they often learn things that don't come out during trials.

Defense lawyers present "mitigation," reasons that a sentence should be lenient. Prosecutors present "aggravation," reasons that a sentence should be harsh.

Sometimes a criminal's violence seems to defy explanation, as if the person were born evil. But often, the hearing reveals a cycle that begins—and ends—with violence.

When defense lawyers argue for light sentences, they often contend that the violence the defendants suffered in the past caused their present violence. Furthermore, they argue that their clients therefore weren't responsible for what they did.

But judges, juries—and the law—rarely accept that. Each person, the law says, is responsible for himself. His past may explain; it doesn't excuse.

Throughout the murder trial of Keith Hoddenbach, any real explanation for Hoddenbach's hateful act remained mysterious. He walked into Max's Red Hots, a near Northwest Side hot dog stand where children were playing video games, and opened fire with a pump shotgun as the youngsters dove for cover.

A street-gang member, Hoddenbach was after a rival. Instead, he murdered a 15-year-old Mexican immigrant named Santos Martinez and injured three others.

His violence was heinous and random; at the sentencing hearing, his lawyer tried to explain it.

The lawyer, Daniel Murray, presented evidence that Hoddenbach's father was an alcoholic who beat his wife and children so badly that the kids once jumped from a second-floor window to escape. Hoddenbach's inner fury solidified when his father raped his sister, who had been very close to him, evidence showed.

"Rather than having support and love, you had violence and hate," Judge Roger Kiley Jr. told Hoddenbach. "The violence that was in your family became part of your bone marrow."

Hoddenbach's past didn't persuade Kiley to be lenient. "Society has to be protected from you," Kiley said, and gave Hoddenbach (who was not eligible for the death penalty) a 110-year prison term; he may be free again, if he lives to be 77.

Demetrius Henderson, another convicted murderer, is on death row awaiting execution. Henderson's 15-page confession, introduced at his trial, is a nightmare of violence. He and another man were convicted of the rape and murder of Kimberly Boyd, a high school student who was repeatedly raped, stabbed more than 30 times, and then run over by a car.

Again, the sentencing hearing revealed what the trial did not. Defense lawyer James Linn presented evidence of Henderson's past: His father was dead—shot and killed before Henderson reached his first birthday. His grandfather was a convicted murderer.

His mother repeatedly flaunted her sexual promiscuity in front of her son; he also witnessed the constant abuse she endured from her string of lovers. Her son was exposed to it all, including the boasts of her most recent boyfriend, who taunted Henderson with details of the tawdry relationship he had with Henderson's mother.

Prosecutors angrily argued that Henderson was "dumping everything at the feet of his mother."

In a recent interview, Judge Richard Neville said he found that Henderson's past led to his crime. "But I didn't find it mitigating," he said. "It led me to believe he was incorrigible, there was so much rage built up in him."

But in the bulk of criminal cases that seem senselessly violent, "it appears to me from my 21 years of experience in this business that there is a connection between violence in your background and the violence you act out," Neville said. "It's almost like a training process."

For Spires, Hoddenbach, and Henderson, the painful cycle of violence is complete. The streets are safe now from these men. But in a corner of the city, where violence is a way of life and a slap across the face substitutes for love, another boy is growing up. And some day he too may have his time in the Criminal Court.

Observations and questions

1) To protect innocent people, Myers fuzzes up some names:

"Many times the police picked up John and Jean, sometimes with their younger sister, Marie, who said she first ran away with them when she was about 6.

"'We would sleep on roofs,' said Marie (both sisters asked that their real names not be used)."

When should we not use names, and how can we compensate for the loss of specificity? Think about all the alternatives to full naming of a character.

2) In the middle of this story about people, Myers has to explain court procedures and judicial theory at length: "A sentencing hearing...it doesn't excuse." Think about how to integrate such information, what Joel Brinkley calls "BBI," Boring But Important. It always interrupts flow, but the reader needs it to understand the story.

3) Myers says she used three cases, rather than just focusing on John Spires, to show a pattern of violent crime arising out of violent family life. Think about this tradeoff of tight and powerful focus on one character versus the diffusion to three. Could she show the pattern convincingly with just one instance?

4) The stories of these three defendants, although not particularly graphic in violent detail, may turn readers off. Study how Myers helps her readers get beyond dismissing Spires, Hoddenbach, and Henderson as monsters. How does she help her readers see them as real people and part of a pattern at the same time?

5) This piece displays commendable restraint in the use of quotations. Notice the apparatus of attribution and contexting required just to get each quotation into the story. Examine each one, and ask whether it would work better as a paraphrase. Can you imagine a story with no quotations at all?

Tour of duty

FEBRUARY 14, 1989

Two young deaf and mute men are charged with burglarizing a school, using a deaf and mute youth as a lookout. The lookout saw police and frantically began to use sign language to warn his accomplices. The burglars didn't get the warning; they were looking the wrong way.

"Thank God, we don't have to prove them smart beyond a reasonable doubt," says a prosecutor watching the burglary case in Criminal Court.

A minister is convicted of stealing expensive suits from Marshall Field & Co. It isn't his first time.

"He knows nine out of 10 commandments," says Thomas Rieck, an assistant state's attorney. "He has a mental block on the other one."

As you spend time here—moving from courtroom to courtroom, floor to floor—you become accustomed to the sights and sounds of the Criminal Court building at 26th Street and California Boulevard. The bungling burglars and the not-so-Christian minister no longer are a surprise. In fact, nothing seems surprising.

The Criminal Court becomes your world as you join those who live here every day. They are judges, lawyers, deputies, clerks, court reporters. Each morning, they stream into the building and bring it to life.

Judge James Bailey and Judge Earl Strayhorn have been on the Criminal Court bench for 18 years, longer than all the other trial judges here.

For all that time, Bailey probably never has stopped being in a hurry. "Come on, come on, come on, let's go, let's go, let's go," Bailey is saying as you walk into his fifth-floor courtroom.

He has no time to waste; he disposed of 1,050 felony cases last year—far more than any other Criminal Court judge.

Bailey is a hard-working, no-nonsense, prosecution-oriented judge. His courtroom has sent more people to death row than any other in the state. From the room's sometimes dingy windows, there's a view of Cook County Jail, just across the street.

Amiable and well-respected, Bailey could only be criticized for being abrupt. Critics say he sometimes agrees to plea bargains too soon, giving defendants lighter sentences than they'd receive if all the facts were heard at trial.

Bailey says he can be fast—and fair—because of his years of experience. At first, it was more difficult to sit in judgment; the first time Bailey sentenced a man to die, he prayed.

"I was concerned, hoping I was following the law, hoping I was doing the right thing, even praying I was doing the right thing," he says. "I must say, it's easier now."

Bailey, slated by the Regular Democratic Organization in 1970, is an Irish-American judge and proud of it. In his judicial chambers, there is a map of Ireland, a St. Patrick's Day parade banner (he wears a green robe on St. Patrick's Day), a shillelagh, and an Irish flag.

For years, the Irish flag was in his courtroom, until a court-watcher's group complained, saying it implied that he would favor a certain ethnic group.

Bailey's parents came from Ireland, where his father had been shot in the leg by the British, he said. They arrived as teen-agers, immigrants who never graduated from grammar school. The flag, to Bailey, is a symbol of his heritage. Banished from the courtroom, it is now in his chambers, near the little statue someone gave him that says "Hanging Judge."

Surrounded by these mementos, Bailey discusses his years in the Criminal Court building. There have been times when he has given the death penalty for a murder, and then has seen a jury in another case refuse to give death for a murder that is even more heinous.

"If you agonize about it, you'll go crazy. You'll have to get out of the building, go do civil work," he says. "I just move on to the next case."

* * *

Near the building's front door, a deputy sheriff is furious. Two families—one the family of an accused murderer, the other of the murder victim—have started fighting in a hallway. "If you're going to fight, fight on the outside," the deputy says. "Don't come in here and fight. Don't ever come in here and fight."

* * *

Like Bailey, the years have made Judge Earl Strayhorn impatient, and taught him to keep tight control over his courtroom.

"Sustained," Strayhorn says, though none of the lawyers in his courtroom has objected. "Sustained, sustained, sustained."

He has heard a lot of posturing by a lot of lawyers at a lot of trials, and there's no need to hear any more.

Strayhorn, dignified and thoughtful, has a way of infuriating lawyers without losing their respect. If he disagrees with a law, he has shown a willingness to challenge it and risk having his ruling overturned by a higher court.

For example, Strayhorn in 1986 stunned many in his courtroom when he refused to obey an Illinois law that mandates a life sentence without parole for anyone convicted of more than one murder. Saying that convicted arsonist Jang Bae didn't "intend to kill anyone"—though his actions resulted in the deaths of three Chicago firefighters—Strayhorn gave him a 70-year prison term instead of life. "You may appeal, cross-appeal," he told prosecutors. "I have sentenced." He was later overturned.

With a certain charm, Strayhorn does verbal battle in his courtroom. During a murder trial, a prosecutor objected to a defense question, saying it was beyond the scope of direct examination. Strayhorn sustained the objection, but the defense lawyer protested.

"I don't think it's beyond the scope, Your Honor," he said.

"I say it is," Strayhorn said. "And I'm what counts."

"Yes, indeed, Your Honor," the lawyer said. He tried again, phrasing his question differently.

"Objection," said the prosecutor, but this time Strayhorn overruled it.

"Oh, he got it in right," the judge said. "Touche, touche."

Another time, Strayhorn said he'd give an accused murderer a 35-year prison term if he pleaded guilty. The defendant wanted 30 years instead, but Strayhorn told him he could take the 35 or go to trial and live with whatever outcome that would hold.

"Roll the dice, brother," the judge told the defendant. "And you better come up 7-11." The defendant took the 35.

Despite his years of confronting criminals, Strayhorn says that "I don't think people are born evil. If I did, I'd give up all hope. I think people have to be taught evil.

"My experience here has taught me the depths to which man can go. How cruel some human beings can be, how uncaring, how callous. And I've also seen the reverse. The heights to which a human being can rise. The dignity, the truth, the caring.

"The whole spectrum of humanity—a kaleidoscope of everything that is human experience—occurs in this building.... I've learned how not to carry the cruelty and inhumaneness. Not to allow that muck and dirt and filth to stay on me."

He does that, he says, by "listening, observing, looking, pondering, praying.... Asking myself, 'Am I allowing the weight of the great awesome powers of wearing these black robes to unduly influence me, so that people aren't being treated fairly and justly?'"

* * *

As you leave Strayhorn's courtroom, you see a lawyer pull his client out of another courtroom. His client, apparently, has forgotten about the Fifth Amendment and has somehow incriminated himself. "As you can see, Joe, there's a definite problem with opening your mouth," the lawyer tells him.

* * *

Unlike other prosecutors, Wayne Meyer rarely raises his voice. This time, he is prosecuting a man accused of leading a brutal gang rape. The victim is so traumatized she has refused to appear in court, but Meyer hasn't told the defense lawyer that.

The judge introduces the defense lawyer to the jury, saying that lawyer represents the accused. Then he introduces Meyer as an assistant state's attorney, who represents the State of Illinois.

Meyer wants to clarify one point. He doesn't represent the State of Illinois—the attorney general does that, he tells the jury. He represents the people of the State of Illinois. That includes you, he says. And it also includes crime victims.

It's not easy to prosecute a rape case without a victim, and most lawyers wouldn't try it. A career prosecutor, it is the more difficult cases that attract Meyer now. In his younger, more idealistic days, he was a probation officer and worked for years in Juvenile Court.

Marijane Placek, an assistant public defender with a reputation for fighting tooth-and-nail for her clients, came here from Juvenile Court also.

With a penchant for gold fingernails and purple high-heeled cowboy boots, Placek's flamboyant dress doesn't mask her love of the law. "There isn't a thing I wanted to be since I was 6 years old but a trial lawyer. I used to think, God, if I could only go before a jury, just once.... My morality is to defend, to do the best for my client, to fight for preservation of the Constitution."

Placek said that when she was transferred here from Juvenile Court, she thought, "God, I'm finally playing the big time. Just let me go into a courtroom. Let me argue a case. Let me take it to the highest degree.

"Then, when I walked in this building—no lie—I met kids I knew in Juvenile Court (as child-abuse victims). That's when it became clear to me. It's history repeating itself, over and over and over."

Meyer says he also saw the horrible backgrounds kids come from, which make them callous and criminal. But once they're formed, they're formed, he says, and all you can do is put them away. Protect society, especially the people who live where crime hits most often: in the poor areas, the ghettos.

Meyer has tried several times to become an associate judge, and he gets high ratings, but hasn't made it. He is not the most politically connected assistant in Richard Daley's office.

At the rape trial, the defense emphasizes that the victim didn't even testify. Then Meyer goes over the horrors of the sadistic gang rape, and softly asks the jurors, "Is it surprising that she's not here?"

A prosecutor for 13 years, Meyer never has lost a jury trial.

Today, the defendant, Paul Williams, is serving time for the rape, in Pontiac Prison.

* * *

Two old men watch a murder case that is being tried again because it was overturned on appeal. The defendant is convicted again of murder, armed robbery, and home invasion. The old men are pleased. "You asked for a new trial," one of them yells to the defendant. "You got it!"

* * *

There are heroes in this building. Minor heroes, unheard of. A boy—the only witness among a dozen with the courage to come forward—helps convict a man of murder. A Cook County Hospital doctor puts her professional reputation on the line, declaring that only child abuse could have caused the burns on a youngster's hands.

Defense lawyers and prosecutors are personal heroes to those whose lives depend on a case; sometimes jurors are too. At a rape trial, Assistant State's Attorney Nicholas Trutenko talks about the victim to the jurors:

"When she was out on the streets, she was alone. But when she walked through that door, she was no longer weak, because in here it is safe. In this building, it is safe and there is justice.... In this building, she has you."

There also are moments of shame, when injustice is done. When a charge against an accused child rapist is dropped because the girl victim is frightened and an inexperienced young prosecutor unintentionally scares her even more, so that she won't talk at all. When a judge—under investigation by a federal probe of judicial corruption—acquits a policeman of all charges, despite testimony from other officers that he fired a gun at them.

You watch as Bennie Williams, a black man, gets the death penalty for killing a youngster to steal his radio.

Then you watch as Charles Hattery, a white man, is spared the death penalty even though he systematically murdered a mother—a black woman—and her two children.

You find yourself glaring at the jurors, furious, wondering, is this justice? And you wonder why you have become so angry at the thought that someone will not die.

* * *

A prosecutor is elated. "Guess what? Guess what?" he is saying, laughing. What is it? A repeat rapist—one he prosecuted and sent to prison—has been killed by a fellow inmate. It makes the prosecutor's day.

* * *

Judge Thomas Maloney yells at a jury for finding an accused rapist innocent. The jurors feel terrible and the defense angrily says it was improper. The rapist attacks another woman several months after the trial. Maloney figured he would. He knew what the rules of evidence kept the jurors from knowing: that the defendant had three prior rape convic-tions. (Prosecuted later for his most recent crime, the defendant is serving life in prison.)

* * *

There's a speech that former prosecutor Thomas Epach used to give at sentencing hearings. It went like this:

"The people who work in this building—the people who have worked here awhile—we see man at his very worst. We see things that people do to each other, that people who never have walked inside this building could only imagine or can't even imagine.

"And there is a way that we human beings are able to cope with that situation, whether it means going home and patting our children on their heads an extra time, or feeling other emotions, or reading another file, moving on to something else, calling the next case...."

As the months pass, the Criminal Court becomes depressing, almost crushing. There seems no end to the ugliness. You wonder: Why does it go on? Why does the violence continue? Is it because it hits hardest in the areas where the poor and powerless live? Is it because the victims become faceless as their numbers grow?

You begin to recognize crime scenes as you pass them in the city. Down that block, a man was shot. In that alley, a body was found. Each becomes a mark on the map in your mind, and then they ripple outward and touch each other and overlap until every part of the city is covered.

It is time for you to leave the Criminal Court. It's late as you walk out for the last time, and people are lining up for Night Bond Court. The streetlights reflect on the wet sidewalks outside. "Be careful," a deputy calls.

When you get home, you'll lock your doors and windows. And if you ever hear a child's scream or a neighbor's cry, you won't be able to stand by and do nothing. For you know now—more than ever—that every child has a face and a smile, and every neighbor has a right to live.

Observations and questions

1) Myers leads with two comic anecdotes. In a series parading the horrors of violent crime, do you find these anecdotes appropriate, especially in such a prominent position? Think about the reader's need for relief and the effect of contrasting comic with tragic stories.

2) Myers describes Judge Bailey's chambers in detail, telling us the history of some of the objects. How does describing the judge's setting help the reader understand some of the difficult things he says?

3) Myers intersperses vignettes of court life among the longer stretches of this story. What purpose do they serve? What would you gain and lose by deleting them?

4) Judge Strayhorn says, "My experience here has taught me the depths to which man can go. How cruel some human beings can be, how uncaring, how callous. And I've also seen the reverse. The heights to which a human being can rise. The dignity, the truth, the caring." Should Myers show us more of the "heights" to balance the "depths"? Would such balance undo her point?

5) After a life sentence is given for a particularly heinous murder, Myers says, "You find yourself glaring at the jurors, furious, wondering, is this justice? And you wonder why you have become so angry at the thought that someone will not die." This kind of naked introspection almost cries out for first-person telling. Is it more effective in the second or the first person?

6) Myers's third story ends like this: "When you get home, you'll lock your doors and windows. And if you ever hear a child's scream or a neighbor's cry, you won't be able to stand by and do nothing. For you know now—more than ever—that every child has a face and a smile, and every neighbor has a right to live." Look back over the entire series and ask yourself if and how Myers has set up this conclusion for the reader.

A conversation with
Linnet Myers

DON FRY: Did you write these court stories on the court beat?

LINNET MYERS: No, I had moved to features. I started writing all the things you can't write when you're doing deadline work. A lot of things you see day to day, small things that might be very meaningful to you, aren't really a news story at all.

Why can't you write about those things on a hard news beat?

For one thing, you don't have time. That beat is very hectic. There are 34 felony courtrooms, and you're running from room to room, trying to make sure you're not missing any big verdicts or sentencings or anything. Many times we did two, three, or maybe even four stories a day.

Also, you can't put in your personal impressions, your feelings, what you're going through when you're watching what other people are going through.

How did you deal with that frustration?

Drank a lot. [Laughter] I was supposed to report the facts, but it was frustrating to see what crime was doing to people. A lot of people in the city and the areas that we cover might not realize this because we had a little 10-inch story in the paper saying, "Joe Schmoe was sentenced Friday to life in prison for the murder of Blah-blah-blah." It was hard to get across how much that meant to the people involved.

How do you deal, day in and day out, with all this parade of human misery, not as a journalist, but as a person?

I wasn't totally kidding when I said I drank a lot....
Every reporter who covered the beat seemed to
handle it in a different way. I found myself getting
angrier and angrier.

**How do you keep from getting hardened and
jaded?**

I didn't get hardened to it, but I got more and more
hostile as each murderer came in.

**Were you able to interview people at length, per-
haps deal with a victim's family?**

Yes. We interviewed victim's families often. Unfortunately, a lot of that was in the hallways of the
court building while the trial was going on inside,
and it wasn't as in-depth as you'd really like. But
sometimes we did have a chance to try to take
some extra time, and you would get to know the
family well, and end up feeling a lot for them.

**Many reporters hate to approach a grieving
family. How do you do that?**

Well, that becomes almost routine, especially when
you figure out that a lot of these families really
want to talk to you. Some of them don't. Sometimes they say, "Get away," and in that case, I'd
usually try again by saying something like, "I'd
like to be able to tell people what your son was
like, why he was an important person, why this
means something that he's dead, and you can tell
me what he was like." If they didn't respond to
that, I'd say, "Fine, goodbye." I'm not going to sit
there and get into an argument with a family whose
son was just murdered.

But most people did want to talk to you?

Yes. I found that when you approached them, told
them what you were doing, most of them wanted
very much to talk about it. They wanted people to

know what their kid was like. They wanted to say how they felt. The average neighbor, friend, whoever, doesn't know how to talk to them, and they might end up feeling pretty isolated a lot of the time, and have a whole lot on their minds that they don't get to express. And in some instances, people would just start talking and talking. In fact, a few times, they would thank me, which seems quite bizarre, because, of course, I should be thanking them, which I did.

Everybody had treated them with kid gloves, and here you come, and you're direct....

Right. Reporters who aren't used to doing this, or who are just starting out, should think to themselves that, in your own small way, you actually help them a little bit to go through it.

With 34 courtrooms in that building, how do you pick out which trials to cover?

You start in the courtroom called "Violence Court."

Is "Violence Court" a nickname or its official name?

That's the official name.

Only in Chicago....

Right. [Laughter] All the murderers and sex criminals go there first, so we would sit there every day, unless something else really big was happening. The facts of each case are read very briefly for a bond hearing, and you get a general idea of the murder, and you can decide which murders are worth following, and which aren't. Generally speaking, for your gang-member-kills-gang-member, you wouldn't bother to follow up. Your husband-kills-wife, wife-kills-husband, you wouldn't do unless it was something like a man killed his wife because she'd been nagging him for 25 years. That you would cover, because that's kind of nice...I mean, that's not nice, but it's...

It's got human interest.

Right. Thank you. [Laughter] But there are certain murders you know the paper is going to be interested in, unusual murders, or something with an unusual angle to it, or a particularly terrible murder, or a multiple murder, or a child-abuse murder.

What do you mean by "unusual" in Chicago?

Well, there are a lot of murders that we call "cheap." We discount these cheap murders, and what we have left is, well, unusual. It's hard for me to say, except maybe by example. We had an old Polish guy, 60-something years old, completely in love with his wife, married like 34 years. The wife dies of cancer. The old guy blames the doctor, stalks down the doctor, and shoots him and kills him.

Wow!

That was a pretty good one. Then some are exceptionally brutal, and those are the ones that are the hardest for me to handle. The really terrible child-abuse murders, where they have burn marks and broken bones and scars, just horrible brutality.

So routine muggings and street shootings don't count.

Yes. That, unfortunately, is not news in Chicago, unless the person who is shot is a very exceptional person. And this is one of my criticisms of my own paper, the *Tribune,* although I think it's true of a lot of papers: If that person is a rich white person, he might get in the paper, but if he's a poor black person, his being shot in the head is not news.

I see. So it isn't really bizarre crime so much as crime that has interesting characters or inter-

esting situations in it, or interesting problems.

Right. Sometimes it's the pettiness of it. We had one murder over a banana pudding pie. Sometimes just the pettiness of what people take each other's lives for is pretty amazing.

Do you take a lot of notes?

Yes, I take more notes than a lot of reporters do. During a trial, if a witness was on the stand, I would try to write down as many direct quotes as I could. Interviewing people in the hall, I tried to get down what they have to say in their own words as much as I could.

Some of your quotations are quite long. Do you use a tape recorder?

I don't tape usually.

Why not?

On that type of deadline writing, we'd be rushing here and rushing there, and when the trials were over and the juries came back, we'd rush down to the press room and start writing, and I wouldn't have time to play back a taped interview. Sometimes you would want to have a tape recorder in the courtroom, but you can't. Some of the judges talk really fast, and the other reporters and I sometimes go up to the court recorders and read to them what we had, just to make sure it was accurate.

But how do you get such long quotations into the notebook?

I have this weird little scrawl that I use. It's not really shorthand, but I abbreviate every word. Then I fill in the blanks there for myself. So "It's frustrating..." would become "it frus." "You know" would be the letter "u" and the word "no." So I can keep up pretty quickly.

I do it that way too, and I have to expand those squiggles pretty soon, or I'll forget what they meant.

Yes, every now and then, I look at my little abbreviation and wonder, "What the heck word is this?" But usually I can remember.

Do you talk over the story with anyone before you write it?

Yes, I call in. I tell the assistant city editors what I want to give them, like, "This was a really good trial. This guy was just found guilty." They'll say, "Okay, give me 15 inches on that." Every now and then, they may say, "Why don't you make that a feature lead?" or, "Why don't you lead with such-and-such?" But that's pretty rare. They usually just say, "Give me the story. So many inches."

How do you organize your notes and materials?

Usually I'll have remembered a few things that stood out in my mind, and I'll right quick find those in the notebook, and put them into the computer. I just start writing at the top of the story, on down through, as fast as I can.

I would write an outline in that situation, but I bet you don't.

No, not at all. I just start writing from the top down.

How do you figure out what the lead is?

The lead, to me, is the unique thing about the story. Otherwise, with a crime story, everything can start sounding like: "An 18-year-old South Side man Tuesday was convicted of the murder of Blah-blah-blah." So I try to get away from that by putting in a quote like, "In a case that a judge said was the most horrendous he had ever heard in his life, a South Side man was convicted..." Or whatever makes the case unique, like the little kid jumping rope who gets caught in the crossfire between two gang members. I'd lead with "Little So-and-so was jumping rope."

It sounds like the things that make you choose something for a lead are the same things that made you choose the story in the first place. It's essentially whatever is newsworthy, or "unusual," as you say in Chicago.

Yes. That's true.

After you have the lead, what do you do next?

Within the first few graphs, I get in the basic information on the case, which sometimes, when you're a reporter, seems a little redundant. You have to put the defendant's age and address, and obviously put in when, who, what, where, get all that up there. And the frustrating thing to me is when that's all you can put in, because there's a lot more to say.

Indeed. Do you revise as you go along, or do you draft and then revise?

I usually write it through once, and then go back over it, and see what might be left out, or what might seem a little awkward, and try to fix that.

How long does it take you to write 10 inches?

A half-hour.

You're pretty fast.

Yes. Maybe it wouldn't take me a half-hour anymore now that I've been in features for a while, but at the time, if my deadline was in a half-hour, I'd write it in a half-hour. [Laughter] If the deadline wasn't for two hours, it might take me an hour.

Were you edited much?

At first, I was edited more. After I had been out there awhile, I gained the trust of the editors, and they didn't edit me as much. But sometimes they do, and you open the paper the next day, and you say, "What the heck is that? This isn't what I wrote." [Laughter]

For this series, did you mine your notebooks from the court beat?

I kept my notebooks in piles by date. And when I got transferred to features, I had these piles of notebooks, dozens and dozens and dozens. The front of the notebook would have some notation to myself of what was in there, and whether something good was in there, and I even put a little star on the ones that I really wanted to remember.

Did you also use the clips?

I had my own clip files by type of crime. When I started out, I had just one file labeled "Murder." And that quickly got so thick that I had to break it into "Murders by Defendants, last names A, B, C, D, blah-blah-blah." And then I also had murders by type. In some cases, I had child-abuse murders separate. I had gang-murders separate. I had cab-driver murders separate, because so many cab drivers get murdered. So if I remembered the type of case, I could pick up that file and find it.

Oooh, I just love organized people. Did you go back through all of that?

I didn't go through everything, because there's a lot. I went through the murder files and the con men. Some defendants were good enough to have their own files, but they were rare.

Did you do any further interviewing?

Yes. A lot of the judges, the public defenders, and the prosecutors were very thoughtful or interesting characters in one way or the other. They might make comments in court that let you know they were really fascinating people. But you can't include in your murder story, day by day, the type of person the judge is, and the way he thinks, and why the way he thinks has affected this particular case.

Why not?

You don't have the space, and it's not really quite appropriate. But for this project, I was able to go back and talk to several of the judges who had intrigued me. I talked to them about a lot of things I wanted to ask them for a long time, like, "What's it like for you to sit up here 20 years, and see murder after murder day after day? How do you deal with it? Do you think you're making any difference? Are you having an impact on crime?" And I did some other interviews with defendants, for instance, John Spires, a child rapist. I went down to the prison and interviewed him at length.

How long did the reporting take for this series?

It's hard to say, because I was working on it between other things, and a lot of it was just going through the incredible amount of notes that I had left over. So that wasn't really reporting so much as reviewing reporting I had already done. I spent about six weeks on it, I would say.

Was the series edited heavily?

No. The first and second parts I wrote were combined into part one quite smoothly. The lead of the second story worked as a good transition anyway. The editors asked for another lead on the first story, and my second try made it.

What was wrong with the first one?

The first one had something like, "Welcome to the Criminal Court where something something...."

They didn't like the "Welcome to..." because they said that's overused. And, to tell you the truth, after that, I did start seeing that "Welcome to..." lead a lot. [Laughter]

See, editors are good for something.

Right.

Your lead starts the series as well as the first piece: "Murderers walk these halls, and the mothers of murderers, and the mothers of the murdered too.
   "This is 26th and California."
   Talk about that lead.

Well, that used to strike me so often: The mothers are very, very present. The mothers of the murderers are just about always behind their kids all the way. Their kids are innocent. They didn't do anything wrong. They were good boys. And they will tell you that, no matter what. The mothers of the murdered are the most incredibly devastated, hurt people, and the pain of violent crime can be seen in them so much, that they seem to me, along with the criminals themselves, the most intense people out there. I hope that makes sense.

Where did the image of the parade come from?

That was my image, because that's really how it seems, especially in Violence Court. You're sitting there, and it's just one after the other, just like some surrealistic parade of grisly or bizarre things. From my frustration covering the day-to-day stuff, I wanted to let the average reader know what it's like to walk through this building, opening a door, seeing an incredible drama going on, closing the door, walking down the hallway again, opening another door, seeing some other incredible thing going on. I was trying to let the reader know what it's like just to be in that building every day, to observe how much is going on, and how intense it is.

You use all sorts of drama imagery. Did you see it that way when you were on the court beat, or did you come up with that later?

I would watch *Perry Mason* or some courtroom drama on TV, and it would strike me, sitting in court, that here it is in real life, and it's so much more real. It is like a drama, like a show, but the emotions are so tense. It's real life and death going on. That makes it a better show than you could ever see on TV, because it's so real.

Indeed, and your writing makes it seem real. Another sentence reads: "Take a seat and watch as defendants are led in from the lockup, one by one." Then the list of people, and what they've done, and the judge reacting, and so forth, gives me a sense of the "parade," as you call it, and the depth of these crimes. You don't tell us too much, but it conjures up a lot.

Well, this was a good day that I used...

Wait.... This is one actual day and not a composite?

Right. They were all on the same day, believe it or not. A composite might have been better, but I wanted an actual day.

I don't think a composite would have been better, because, as you say, the real is so real here. Speaking of reality, I want to ask you a question about court reporting in general. The average citizen does not understand how the courts work. In fact, many beginning reporters don't know how the courts work.

Right. [Laughter]

So when you don't have much space, how do you work in what the reader needs to know about court procedure? For example, you say:

"Next, Reginald Morgan, charged with sexual assault. Defense lawyer Thomas Breen objects because Morgan has been *indicted by a grand jury without a preliminary hearing,* at which the defense could present its case. The objection is routine, but today Breen decides to add a little emphasis. 'We're shocked,' Breen says.

"'For the record, he's shocked,' says the judge. "

Lots of tough jargon for the reader in there.

Explanation is very hard to do, and a lot of times, we just don't put it in. Unfortunately, the average person might be a little confused, but it's so wordy and technical-sounding to explain courtroom procedures. Almost any reporter who starts over there doesn't know what the heck is going on. It takes awhile to figure out what type of hearing this is, and what happens next, and what an indictment means, and what's a preliminary hearing as opposed to an indictment, and all that.

In this case, we put this sentence in here hoping people would understand it. I just wanted to show that, even when the crime is really serious, these lighthearted, weird exchanges go on between lawyers and judges as part of the scene, because everyone is so used to what's going on there.

As a reader, I'm grateful for the funny bits. If you hadn't put them in, I would have read this endless parade of misery, a real downer. But I can see these people as people, because you present them as funny.

That's probably why they joke around so much, because the judges and lawyers couldn't stand the constant misery either. And some of the crimes are just so absurd. Take this guy in the aquarium feeling up this little girl; the judge just naturally starts joking about that. I hope that doesn't sound too bizarre.

No, not *too* bizarre. Let's talk about handling

dialect and non-standard grammar in quotations. Look at this passage:

"One day a man named Andre Collins was brought in after being picked up on a warrant for an armed-robbery murder. The paperwork was in duplicate; Judge Bolan announced that Collins was charged with two murders.

"Collins didn't react at all when the first charge was read, but he wasn't ready to accept two. 'Uh-uh,' he objected. *'Wasn't no two.'* Spectators giggled, and Judge Bolan turned his chair around, broke into laughter, and turned back again a moment later, his face red."

Sometimes we correct grammar. If you're interviewing a reasonably educated person who makes a grammatical error now and then, you would probably give that person a break and correct it. But when you get this guy, this armed robber, hauled in, and he says, "Wasn't no two," I couldn't possibly say that any better than he said it. I could say, "It wasn't two," but...

Then you lose the anecdote.

Right. He said it so perfectly, succinctly, and in his own way, and I wouldn't want to change that.

But quoting dialect may look like condescension.

Yes, I can see that. But I don't feel condescending toward the defendants, and sometimes I actually admire their way of talking, because it's very colorful and interesting and can be more vivid than someone who talks properly. I hope readers realize that we're not trying to insult the defendants here. We're just trying to present them here for what they are, for how they are.

Fine. A couple of paragraphs down, Judge Bolan says: "It's frustrating, you know, that tomorrow there's going to be a whole new batch.... It's of a continuing nature. You'd like to see

some kind of reward, and *there's no clear lines* here of any reward."

He should have said: "There are no clear lines." Were you tempted to clean up his grammar? You didn't clean up the guy above, Andre Collins...

That's true.

...but he's a murderer. [Laughter]

Yes, and I didn't clean the judge up either. If the person has his natural way of talking, sometimes I just like to leave that in there. I don't remember my editors asking if I wanted this quote corrected. I think I just decided to let him talk the way he talks. If you write down everything I say exactly as I'm saying it, there's going to be some mistakes, but sometimes that makes the person sound more natural and more human.

Indeed. In editing these conversations for *Best Newspaper Writing*, I sometimes leave some of the fillers in just to make it sound like speech. And the interviewee will call me up and say something like, "Well, everything in the conversation is just fine, but I notice that *you* start a lot of *my* sentences with 'Well.'" [Laughter] You have Judge Bolan saying "you know" in the beginning of that paragraph.

Yes. I leave a lot of "well's" in. If someone says "you know" or "well" or something like that, you can hear them talking. It seems more natural.

Well, I want you to remember, you know, what you just said when you read this conversation in the book.

Okay. [Laughter]

Let's talk about your amazing "rules" passage, which starts like this:

"With time, you begin to learn the rules of the Criminal Court. Some are rules of law and evidence. Others are unwritten rules.

"There's the Criminal Court rule of motherhood: Mothers will lie for their children. A mother will swear to tell the truth and then testify that her son was with her, when he was in fact committing murder."

How did you come up with that wonderful device?

Well, it began to strike me as I was in that building month after month, that there are a lot of unwritten things that go on and that fit into categories. Prosecutors will even say, "Well, you know the rule. This is child-abuse killing. I won't get more than a manslaughter verdict." Things start falling into patterns: Here is another mother telling me her kid is innocent, another mother who doesn't believe fingerprints and eyewitness testimony and a signed confession. You know the same thing is going to happen, as if they were rules, although obviously they're not written down.

I'm most struck by the end of your rules section:

"Rules say the murder of a 'dirty victim'— like a gang member or a vagrant—isn't good, but it's not as bad as the murder of a 'clean victim.' Rules say there's no sexism, but it's easier to get off if you're a woman.

"Rules say there's no racism, but if you want to escape the death penalty, statistics indicate it's probably better to murder a black person than a white person."

You're saying some pretty harsh stuff here.

Yes. The editors and I discussed this part, especially the racism one, and it was slightly changed. I wrote: "If you want to escape the death penalty, it's better to murder a black person than a white person," which the editors changed to *"statistics indicate it's probably better* to murder a black person than a white person," which is fine with me, because statistics do indicate that, and maybe that makes it stronger.

No, I think it makes it weaker. The phrase "statistics indicate" is generic attribution, and it's pulling the punch on *your* observation.

Well, that's what they wanted to do. They were uneasy with me because I out-and-out said it's better. I would like to be able to say it's better because I observed it time and time again, and I know it's true. When the editors told me they had a problem with this, that's what I argued to them, and they said, "Well, we're going to put in there 'statistics indicate.'"

It was okay with me because, first of all, I got the point in, and if they feel it's too risky a thing to say without some kind of attribution, then maybe that's what the paper has to do. Come to think of it, though, it's kind of weird that they let me say it's easier to get off if you're a woman. I don't think any statistics indicate that.

Maybe your editors are men.

Right. [Laughter]

For a court reporter in a situation like this, or any person writing a story like this, how do you avoid stereotyping? Did you worry about that?

Not really, because after you're over there long enough, stereotypes do kind of fall away, because you get to know everyone on a pretty individual level, just by watching his trial.

I'm less worried about you than about the reader. We have here a parade of villains, and a lot of them are black or Hispanic. Because of the way we present news, readers are pounded with this constant message that minorities commit crimes. That notion can easily turn into: Most crimes are committed by minorities. Eventually

**you get to: Most minorities are criminals. Do
you worry about the reader drawing conclusions like those?**

Yes, I do. We do not get across well enough to readers, particularly to rather sheltered people who
don't really deal with city life all the time, that these
crimes are going on in the ghettos, and they always
have, and certain things cause people to commit
crime. It's not because they're black or Hispanic;
it's certain conditions. In the era of waves of Irish
immigration here in Chicago, it was all Irish names
committing crimes; and then all Italian names; and
now they're black and Puerto Rican. But the ghetto
is always the source of crimes about money. I think
we should get across that the average crime *victim* is
black or Hispanic and poor. They're good people.
They're hard-working people. They live in a really
bad neighborhood. They have to deal with this every
day.

Crime is a real fear among a lot of poor people,
black people, and Hispanic people, and we're not
getting that across as much as we're getting across
that the people who are victimizing them are black.
If I called and said, "I have here a story about a repeat rapist in the Inglewood neighborhood who has
committed 20 home-invasion rapes," the desk is not
going to be very interested. Inglewood is a poor,
black, ghetto neighborhood on the South Side. But
if it's 20 rich, white women in Wilmette, a rich suburb, they're going to love it. And it might be a
black rapist in both cases.

News is white news.

Yes. That aggravated me many, many times. I'd
call up the next day and ask, "Why didn't this story
get in?" And they'd say, "Well, it was a busy news
day," or something like that. Maybe it was a busy
news day, but I feel there is a pattern in that.

**Let's look at the second story, "Born losers."
You focus on Mr. Spires. Were there other can-**

didates you rejected as the central character of this piece?

I considered a few, and I briefly mentioned these other two guys in the story. Spires really fit what I was trying to say, and his crimes were so incredibly heinous, even worse than a murderer, because people think of a child rapist as totally inhuman. I thought that confronting the most repulsive might be effective in getting the point across.

And I'll bet you had a lot of good stuff on how he got the way he is.

That's true. Some of the stuff came out at the sentencing hearing, especially his psychiatric records. He was very interesting to interview, and his sisters were also very open. They were willing to talk about it, whereas a lot of people are not willing to talk about their families in a negative way, or about abusive parents.

I found this section describing Spires rather frightening, especially the man's desperation. He goes so far as to ask for a lobotomy. It's very powerfully written, with good detail.

Thank you. That wasn't hard, because just letting him talk was pretty powerful. I went down to Menard Prison and sat with him for a few hours. He has so much pain and self-hatred, and so much conflict and misery inside, and that's really the core of his violence. Now don't get me wrong. I think this guy should be locked up forever and ever. I think he's a horrible, horrible person, and I'm glad he will never get out again.

I wondered why you didn't stick with Spires. Why did you bring in two more cases?

I did think about that question, one person versus three, before writing it. Focusing on one person can be the most dramatic way of getting your point across, but I thought, "The reader might think this is one isolated guy from a really bad background." But I also wanted to get across the fact that this seems to be a pattern. And with the other two cases, we had very experienced Criminal Court judges who commented that they have seen this pattern again and again. I liked Judge Kiley saying, "Rather than having support and love, you had violence and hate. The violence that was in your family became part of your bone marrow." That really struck me. So I decided to throw in the other two guys.

Let's look at your ending:
"For Spires, Hoddenbach, and Henderson, the painful cycle of violence is complete. The streets are safe now from these men. But in a corner of the city, where violence is a way of life and a slap across the face substitutes for love, another boy is growing up. And some day he too may have his time in the Criminal Court."
Good kicker.

Thanks. Every time I see a survivor, like a brother or sister, of a child-abuse murder victim, or a survivor of severe child abuse, I look at that kid and think, "He's going to be back here in 10 years behind bars." I started thinking that if we want to stop this type of horrible, senseless violence, we have to start dealing better with child abuse. I wanted to get across that point, because I think that's one of the main things wrong with life today in this country. Kids are brutalized, and they're becoming hardened and evil and violent. One of the advantages of writing features is you can end with impressions. I liked being able to put some of my feelings in.

You lead the third story with the two deaf mutes and the minister who stole suits. Why did you pick that lead?

Because it's just so bizarre. There are just so many weird little wacky things that happen in the day-to-day life in the court building.

I liked that lead, because it was a funny lift after all the heavy tragedy in that last story.

I wanted to make sure that the human, funny, ironic side of the courts came across as much as the real hard-core violent side, because both of those are always happening there.

Very late in the piece, you say, "You find yourself glaring at the jurors, furious, wondering, is this justice? And you wonder why you have become so angry at the thought that someone will not die."
You're getting pretty naked there.

I was trying to get across what starts happening to your mind when you're overwhelmed with this type of thing. This actually happened to me and another reporter. I was becoming angrier, more on edge, more tense, more demanding of justice, more outraged, and it was just building, building, building. When you deal with this every day, you get really wound up, to the point where you start wanting vengeance, and you start getting a little bit out of control. In this series, I was trying to put the reader in the shoes of someone who's hanging out there all the time.

This particular case, when the jury came back with no death penalty for Charles Hattery, was one of my more embarrassing moments. A guy owed the gang money. And they came over to the guy's house and insisted on the money, and the guy said, "Okay. I'll take you there." He went off with a couple of the guys, and they left Charles Hattery there with the wife and her two little bitty children. They said, "If we're not back at 8:00, kill them." So at about five to 8, Charles starts ticking off the seconds on his digital watch, telling the woman, "Two more minutes. One more minute. Thirty more seconds." And then he murdered her little bitty baby in the crib, her little 2-year-old, and then her.

Yikes!

This was a white man killing a black woman and her two children. If anybody deserves the death penalty, why didn't he get it? I was standing there with another reporter when the jury came back with no death penalty. We always interview the jurors. And I found myself in that moment...this sounds kind of bad...I found myself in that moment so angry with them...this is how far gone I was... [Laughs] I was so angry at them that I was afraid to ask them a question, because my question would have been, "What type of asshole are you that you let this guy off?!" And you're not supposed to ask that. So we just stood there, I and the other reporter, who was just as angry as I was, and just watched them go by us, and didn't even interview them, which was totally stupid and not very professional. And that's when it was starting to dawn on me that I'd better get out of that beat.

Indeed. How do you know when to get off the court beat? What are the signs?

For me, the signs were that I was just getting so wound up, when I started feeling that the next child molester I saw, I was going to slap him, or something. [Laughter] I was also becoming the most cautious citizen in the city of Chicago, checking locks and looking behind me.

And when you say to a good editor, "I'm burned out," he's going to listen to you.

I would think so, yes.

Yours did.

Yes.

Let's look at the end of the story, and of the series:
"When you get home, you'll lock your doors and windows. And if you ever hear a child's scream or a neighbor's cry, you won't be able to

stand by and do nothing. For you know now—
more than ever—that every child has a face and
a smile, and every neighbor has a right to live."
  Is that the point of the story?

Yes, definitely. In the day-to-day coverage of crime,
we miss that these people are individuals. They're
each important in themselves. They each have
something to offer someone. They're loved by
somebody. They're not just a name in the paper, or
a statistic. We should care about them. And that's
what I was trying to say there.

You said it long before you got there, and that
final paragraph underlines it. Well, Linnet, you
know how you reporters save the hard question
for the end?

Yes...

Here comes the hard one. The court beat is a parade of human misery, as you put it here, and
you have to write it fast. Even writing a series
like this one is hard, and gets you involved in a
lot of tough decisions and emotions.

Yes...

Is it fun?

[Laughter] It's really fun. As bizarre as that sounds,
it's fun because it's constant action, always something different. There are always things going on
around you. You're never bored. You're just always
going, going, and it's a very intense life, and it's ex-
hilarating. Although you have to deal with a lot of
things emotionally, and you see a lot of terrible
things, there's this action and drama going around
you all the time that's really fascinating.

A great beat, but not for too long, right?

That's what I would say.

The Boston Globe

Wil Haygood
Finalist, Non-Deadline Writing

From his position as feature writer for *The Boston Globe,* Wil Haygood has written about the political climate in South Africa, rural poverty in Alabama, the prison lifestyle of singer James Brown, and the declining years of former U.S. Congressman Carl Elliott. Haygood's writing was cited as a factor in Elliott's selection in 1990 for a JFK: Profile in Courage Award. Born in Columbus, Ohio, Haygood became a journalist after earning a degree in urban studies from Miami University of Ohio. He worked for the *Columbus Call & Post, Charleston* (W.Va.) *Gazette,* and *Pittsburgh Post-Gazette* before joining the *Globe* in 1984. He won the National Headliners Award for feature writing in 1986 and was an Alicia Patterson Foundation Fellow in 1988.

The story on Thomas Hardeman reprinted here is the sidebar to an article on a tragedy that happened 33 years ago. Haygood traveled throughout the South and East, and tracked down former Marine company members and relatives to present a quiet story on unending sorrow.

'He was so proud to be a Marine'

NOVEMBER 2, 1989

SAVANNAH, Ga.—Most of his life Thomas Hardeman worked on farms, sharecropping.

"That's all he knew," Eugene Hardeman says of his brother. "He lived out here on Fort Stewart with a man and his daughter. He was kind of sweet on the farmer's daughter." Nothing ever happened. When it was time to go, it wasn't about the farmer's daughter, but the next paycheck.

Money came slow in those days, and it seemed to get away quicker than sawdust in a storm. So Thomas Hardeman, who had always sent some money home to his family, set his sights on joining the Marine Corps. He failed the first test and he failed the second test. But he didn't know how to quit. He could plow a field all day by himself. Surely he could pass a military test. On the third try he passed. Then he left for Parris Island.

"He was so proud to be a Marine," says Eugene Hardeman. "My mother went over twice, on Sundays, to see him. He was a poor ol' farm boy trying to make something of himself is what it amounted to. He was gritting his teeth and taking it. He never let on to Mother that it was difficult over there."

Mother was Maggie Meeks, a Depression-era woman who had to raise her five boys, alone, when her husband was found dead on the couch from what, in those days, was called a leaking heart.

"She came up the hard way on the farm," Eugene Hardeman says. "For three years she kept five boys together. She didn't put us in no orphan home or nothing."

Maggie Meeks stacked peanut hay for 25 cents a day. Relatives wondered how long she could keep that up. Not long after her first husband died, family friends came over with Tom Meeks, who lived in the area and worked over at Georgia-Pacific Plywood. Tom Meeks had a little money in his pockets.

"She needed somebody to help raise the kids," Eugene Hardeman says. "He needed a place to stay. Neither of them loved each other." They married anyway. "They grew to love each other," Eugene Hardeman figures. They stayed together until Tom Meeks died and Maggie Meeks had to put another husband in the ground.

This is "sweet onion" country. Eugene Hardeman has a half-acre of it, far enough away from downtown Savannah to let you know you're in the country. His house sits back off the curve of an unmarked road. At night, when the woods and roads go dark, it would take endurance to find his place. But right now the morning sun is up, and there's a dog in the yard. The dog's name really is Patches. Next to his master Patches is gentle, childlike. But not long ago a policeman came by, something about a traffic summons, and opened the gate without calling out to Eugene Hardeman. Patches went for the policeman's ankle and drew blood.

Eugene was the baby brother; Thomas the older brother who always looked out for him. They were close.

On the night of the drownings, Maggie Meeks received a telegram that her boy was missing. "I said I knew Thomas was a good swimmer," says Eugene Hardeman, who sat beside his mother, hoping that his brother "got on one of those marsh islands." When they were little boys, Thomas and Eugene Hardeman used to go swimming. Thomas was so good. But every now and then he'd get muscle cramps and would break through the surface of the water as if he had been stung by a bee. It never happened when he was in water over his head, says Eugene Hardeman, so he always managed to wave for help. Maggie Meeks sat there with that telegram while other family members drew up close. Two days passed, and still no Thomas. Then a scuba diver, on the third day, when everyone had begun to think Thomas might not ever be found, that the swamp and the ocean beyond had claimed him, looked up through goggles and saw a hand sticking up out of the water, like a little white flag, almost as if to wave him over.

Eugene Hardeman figures, inasmuch as Thomas Hardeman was a powerful swimmer, that he must have been trying to save another boy—platoon members had testified that he saved at least two boys that night—and caught muscle cramps. From the waist up, the swamp crabs had pretty much eaten away at Thomas Hardeman. His entire body had to be wrapped in white gauze. You couldn't see any flesh as he lay there in the casket. Eugene Hardeman had walked up to the casket, a solid copper casket the Marines paid for, and noticed a little red spot on his brother's forehead. It looked like a red raindrop. He figured a wound must have opened up.

The good die young.

"He had guts," said Matthew McKeon, Hardeman's drill instructor. "You could tell he had guts."

"My mother could hear that for years, and turn off like a television set," Eugene Hardeman says about taps, the bugle call played at the funeral. Even now, says Eugene Hardeman's wife, Elizabeth, her husband will be watching something on television, and that bugle call will come on, and he'll painfully lift himself out of the chair and walk outside. She'll go looking for him, pushing past the screen door, and find him around the side of the house, telling her he's all right, trying to keep his hands from his eyes, telling her to go on back inside, the dog right there at his knee.

"I just wonder," says Eugene Hardeman, "what Thomas would have turned out to be. You know, you just wonder about things like that."

Anchorage Daily News

Charles Wohlforth
Finalist, Deadline Writing

Charles P. Wohlforth was born in New York and grew up in Anchorage. After spending a year working in public radio, he went to Princeton University and earned a degree in English literature and creative writing. In 1986, he began reporting at the *Homer* (Alaska) *News,* and two years later he joined the *Anchorage Daily News*, a McClatchey newspaper. Wohlforth was stationed in a bureau when he was asked to cover the Valdez oil spill. He spent months covering a story that was a seven-hour drive from his home in Anchorage.

His stories make sense of a complicated, unorganized scene. They bring out the emotions involved in an environmental tragedy. Most of all they let the reader see, hear, feel, touch, and smell the things that Wohlforth and others on the scene confront.

Rescuers work hard, but catch is small

APRIL 1, 1989

HERRING BAY, Alaska—World attention focused Friday on the attempt to rescue birds and animals from the oil spilled in Prince William Sound. Cameras in Valdez focused on the few animals saved— fewer than 20 birds and four sea otters by evening Friday. The birds on the evening news were expensive symbols for Exxon, costing more than $1,000 apiece to rescue.

But on the water, the rescue efforts getting all the attention stumbled along with the air of a Sunday outing. In this bay at the north end of Knight Island, a diverse and committed group of people tried to learn to perform a futile task.

Jim Merritt is learning a new skill. He's used to driving his 31-foot jet boat in the surf of eastern Prince William Sound to catch salmon. Now he is learning to chase ducks.

Merritt's boat caught six birds. Thursday and the first half of Friday, the four-boat flotilla of which it was a member caught 10, one of which died soon after.

About twice as many were found dead, and many times that number were found oiled but could not be captured. Workers elsewhere in the Sound caught about half a dozen birds, and a helicopter pilot grabbed two.

The wake behind Merritt's boat was black in some spots. The rocky shores of the bay were painted black with oil. The smell of oil off the water was strong enough to make some bird workers feel dizzy and ill.

Big snowflakes fell and, for a moment, stuck unmelted on the oily surface.

Merritt, who is young, affable, and able to maneuver his boat like a forklift, had his doubts about the effort the group was putting into catching the birds and the danger it posed to the aluminum boat he built a year ago, and is still struggling to pay for. He said the $2,000-a-day plus fuel costs he is being paid by Exxon does not compensate for the wear and tear.

A pair of cormorants flew out of a crack on the shore. Merritt nosed the boat close and Terry McCambly jumped off on the steep, oil-coated rock. Tim Warrick balanced high on the boat's gunwale to poke a dip net into the hole. McCambly clung to the cliff hoping to catch a bird on its way out the other side of the cave. A rock overhang threatened to smash the windows and headlights of Merritt's boat.

No bird came out. After two hours of trying such efforts—chasing birds through the water only to see them dive, then watching their bubbles—the catchers had only a plastic bag full of already-dead murres and ducks.

An eagle hung in the misty air around the steep, forested shore. Nicolette Heaphy, the only one of the Berkeley, Calif., International Bird Rescue Research Center's three staff members on board, watched the eagle through foggy glasses.

"Anything that's in bad enough shape for us to get, the eagles have probably got already," she said.

But McCambly was not downhearted. He had been planning since the night before, preparing a throw net and putting an extension on a sport fishing dip net.

On shore the oil mixed with algae, and men in rubber boots and rain gear were at its mercy, sliding into tide pools and balancing precariously over the icy, oily water.

But McCambly alone seemed to have a special talent for the work—a tenacity and balance that allowed him, with the long-handled net, to sneak up on nearly catatonic ducks and nab them. Even he couldn't catch birds that had much life left in them.

Unlike the Californians and kayakers on board, who eat avocado, cucumber, and bean sprout sandwiches, McCambly is a gritty 30-year-old fisherman of four continents with an open enthusiasm for the most graphic of pornographic magazines.

He owns three fishing boats. "I got a really good

deal on my boats, I spent most of my money on drugs," he said. "I went through 36 grand in six weeks. I spent half my money on women, half my money on drugs. Not anymore though. Now I spend all my money on women."

But it doesn't take an idealist to want to rescue the birds. McCambly thinks it is worth Exxon's money, although he says workers like himself should be paid more than the $150 a day plus expenses they have been receiving.

"Birds have no fault in this," McCambly said, "and Exxon, if it costs them $1,000 a bird, they ought to pay it. If it costs them $100,000 a fish, they should pay it."

So far, it probably has cost Exxon at least $1,000 for each of the birds, not members of endangered species, which have been saved.

The fleet of bird catchers numbers four boats being leased for $2,000 a day each or more. The skipper of the largest boat said his contract with Exxon forbade him to talk to reporters. There were seven untrained workers and a group of three experts. They sent 11 birds and one otter to a bird hospital in Valdez in a helicopter that rented for $1,650 an hour. The trip took two hours.

In publicity alone the birds may have been worth their cost to Exxon, because they showed that something was being done. Photographers, mostly shore-bound, literally fought to get a look at them.

Thursday evening a pair of photographers got into a tussle trying to take pictures of one of three birds that had been rescued, among a mob that was trying to get a shot. A British photographer kicked a *Fairbanks Daily News-Miner* photographer, who fell and almost crushed the bird when he landed on top of Jessica Porter, who was holding it.

Rescuers in Herring Bay were unaware of the chaos on shore.

Cordova bookstore owner Kelley Weaverling planned to head back to Cordova and get more help.

"My feeling is that we're going to have to get lots more boats," said Jay Holcomb, co-director of the bird center, Exxon's consultants. "We're going to have to call in and say get us 40 boats with four people on each."

Weaverling has organized the entire expedition. "I can take one of the seiners, go to Cordova, gather a fleet, and come back with them," he told Holcomb.

Holcomb acknowledged that the effort receives the expensive support because it gives Exxon good publicity.

Yet the workers seem entirely sincere in their efforts. They love the Sound and want to try to save it, even if their efforts are insignificant compared to the enormity of the disaster.

Weaverling spends four months of each summer kayaking on the Sound. He said Friday morning that he hadn't had time to react to what he had seen since he got out on the oily water Thursday.

Asked what he thought, he started to cry.

"When I woke up we were here in Herring Bay and it was real thick," he said. "It's like you've come home and everything you own is totally defiled. There's s--t everywhere, there's graffiti on the wall, there's vomit and urine everywhere, all your favorite things are smashed. It's beyond irresponsible. It's criminal."

And then he set back to work.

Elwin Johnston, an Anchorage paralegal, caught a sea otter.

Johnston and two others were in a skiff when they saw four otters. Three were in the oily water and escaped, but one was on the snow above the shore, rolling in a patch of snow and trying to clean the mucouslike oil from his fur.

Cannery worker Phil King circled around into the woods while Johnston stood at the shore with a net. When the otter fled King, Johnston caught it.

"I got him with a long net, just like a good center fielder," Johnston effused, as the otter, by then named Oscar, scarfed down herring.

Another otter was caught by cleanup workers, who put it in a duffel bag. One that could not move was caught by a helicopter that flew in specially.

Heaphy cooed to the birds as they were caught, wrapped in pieces of bed sheet, and placed in boxes. She talked to them when she took them out of the boxes to push a tube—catheter for humans—down their throats, and injected a cherry-flavored nutrient solution made for human babies directly into their stomachs.

But for all her gentleness, Heaphy knew that the group is not saving Prince William Sound. Contrary to prevailing opinion in Valdez, away from the action, the rescuers knew that what they were doing was a gesture made because they have kind hearts.

"Life is unfair," Heaphy said. "We're just getting the lucky ones. It's a very special set of circumstances that lets a bird be sick enough that we can catch it, but not dead."

By Friday afternoon, about two miles of the shore of Herring Bay had been thoroughly searched.

Only a few thousand left to go.

The Times Herald
RECORD

Mike Levine
Finalist, Commentary

Life as a New York songwriter convinced Mike Levine that he was better suited for journalism. In his first
year as a journalist, he became editor of a weekly
and won a state press award for column writing.
Levine was born in New York City and studied
American history at City College. After quickly
moving up to editor of the *Heights-Inwood,* a weekly
in north Manhattan, Levine saw an ad for a position
at *The Times Herald-Record* and applied. He started
as a feature writer there in 1980 and is now associate
editor and columnist. The paper is part of the Ottaway Newspaper chain and has a circulation of about
90,000.

Levine's columns show the power of the pen, or
computer terminal, in bringing daily joys and trials
before the community. Here he allows a baby's cry
to scream out against problems and injustices in
medical treatment.

Baby's agony enough to make you scream

OCTOBER 11, 1989

On the morning of April 14, 1989, Jennifer Shickle howled into the world. The nurse brushed the baby against her mother's pale face. The father's smile all but shone through the surgical mask.

The doctor told them, good news, the baby's fine except she has a birthmark in a spot no one will ever see.

Her parents took her home to their Monticello apartment. It wasn't long before Jennifer cooed and smiled and slept through the night.

When she was 3 months old, the birthmark began to swell. It flared to an angry red blotch from the top of her backside to her anus. Jennifer screamed.

They took Jennifer to one doctor who suggested antibiotic cream. Then another doctor who said it would clear up by itself. Another said they should put compresses on her. Yet another suggested a colostomy. The next doctor said that wouldn't be a good idea.

Jennifer continued to cry. The sore festered. An ulcer opened. She bled.

They took her to a specialist at New York University Hospital in Manhattan. He said he had never seen anything like this. The birthmark was called hemangioma. And, as a matter of fact, NYU was holding a conference about it. They could take Jennifer there.

Two days before Jennifer went to the conference, her father was laid off from his construction job.

She went to the conference Sept. 28. Eight doctors handled her, ripping apart the cheeks of her backside to examine her. She screamed in pain. Her mother screamed. They had the parents sign a release, saying it was okay to use pictures of Jennifer's rear end for their own purposes.

They charged her parents $75 for the pictures.

Then the doctors conferred and said a new laser

therapy might help. Surgery was scheduled for Oct. 12, to be performed by a plastic surgeon named Glen Jelks.

The bleeding got worse. Jennifer could not sleep for more than 10 minutes at a time. Her parents took turns rocking her. Then she would howl again. They tried to bathe her. She hurt too much to even sit.

They called the doctor. He decided it was too urgent to wait. He moved the surgery up to Oct. 9, this past Monday.

A woman from Jelks's office named Debbie told them the fee was $2,500. Jennifer's mother said they had Medicaid. We don't take Medicaid, said Debbie.

Can you come up with half? No, said Jennifer's mother. My husband is temporarily out of work, but we are honest people and we will set up a payment schedule.

Sorry, Jennifer's parents were told. Try calling a clinic. Jennifer's surgery was canceled. Goodbye.

That is how Jennifer Shickle's parents remembered it yesterday, before I called Dr. Jelks's office.

A woman named Michele answered the phone. She could not say anything because Jennifer wasn't a patient.

Was surgery canceled, I asked.

She said the surgery appointment was "a mistake."

Was it because of money?

You'll have to contact the patient, said the woman from the doctor's office.

The patient, 6 months old, has stunning blue eyes. She lies limp on her mother's shoulder, seemingly exhausted from her tears and her screams. She starts a smile. In the spot where most babies might have a small diaper rash, Jennifer is branded with a blood-purple rash. Suddenly, the smile is interrupted by a howl.

Three hours after my call to Jelks, a woman from his office called Jennifer's parents. There had been a mix-up, she said. The doctor would reschedule the surgery. She said it would cost them practically nothing.

The big mistake, of course, is that a 6-month-old baby must depend on a doctor's good will or a newspaper's phone call to have her pain soothed. Americans—from babies to the elderly— are condemned to sickness and death because they do not have the money.

I have heard all the arguments about national health insurance. They crumble to dust before one baby's scream.

Sun-Sentinel

Tom Kelly
Finalist, Editorial Writing

Tom Kelly was a journalism administrator for 14 years, doing only occasional writing. A native of Allentown, Pa., he earned a degree in journalism from Lehigh University in Bethlehem, Pa. His professional career began in 1958 at the Allentown *Morning Call* where he was a general assignment reporter. During the nearly three decades that followed, he worked as sports writer or sports editor at the *Florida Times Union,* the *St. Petersburg Times,* and the St. Petersburg *Evening Independent.* He was also managing editor, then editor, of the *Palm Beach Post.* In 1987 Kelly took a year off from journalism. He joined the *Fort Lauderdale News/Sun-Sentinel* editorial board in 1988.

Kelly's editorials deride the ridiculous, whether it is found in the actions of major government officials, powerful companies, or individual citizens.

Reagan's trip to Japan demeaning

OCTOBER 27, 1989

Surely Ronald and Nancy Reagan don't need the money. Book royalties alone will keep them well-supplied with hair dye and designer clothes for the rest of their days.

Why then are the former president and first lady demeaning the highest office the United States can bestow in their shameless $2 million personal-appearance tour of Japan?

If it's the media spotlight the Reagans crave, they hardly needed to fly halfway around the world to find it. Reagan's recent brain surgery and the publication of his wife's venomous memoirs have kept them at the forefront of American consciousness.

If it's a longing for recognition as a global statesman, Reagan needn't have bothered. His monumental accomplishment of beginning a new dialogue with the Soviet Union will live in the history books long after his embarrassing lecture circuit of Japan is forgotten.

If he is allowing himself to be manipulated by the giant Fujisankei Communications Group as a payoff for past services rendered, Reagan at least could have had the decency to decline a fee for his nine days' work, especially a sum so obscene that it surpasses his total salary for eight years as president.

Americans deserve more from their ex-presidents. Jimmy Carter, who devotes his life to mediating regional disputes and studying global problems, is a much better role model. Even the disgraced Richard Nixon, who still offers cogent advice on foreign affairs, exhibits more dignity in retirement than Reagan.

But The Gipper is only being consistent. No one should be surprised that a man who once shared movie billing with a chimpanzee would continue making a monkey of himself in his dotage.

The Hartford Courant

Mark Pazniokas
Finalist, Gov't. Reporting

The path into journalism was a direct one for Mark Pazniokas. He grew up in Norwood, Mass., earned a degree in journalism from Boston University in 1979, and started working for the *Journal Inquirer,* a suburban daily in Manchester, Conn. In three years he moved from general assignment to covering state government, and opened the paper's first state bureau. In 1984 he joined the *Hartford Courant* to cover city hall before returning to state capitol coverage.

His stories show how a legislature really works, or as he says, "how reality differs from the public's perception. I write about the way the legislature operates by the seat of its pants as opposed to the images in civic textbooks," Pazniokas said.

Judiciary panel works as the night wears on

APRIL 10, 1989

The State Capitol and Legislative Office Building are nearly deserted. The yellow school buses that park bumper to bumper on Trinity and Elm streets during the day are long gone.

It is 8 p.m. Thursday. The tour guides in the red blazers gave their last how-a-bill-becomes-law speech to visiting students hours ago. The young children are safely home, fed, and ready for bed.

Now it is time for the adults to go to work. Deadlines are approaching, and the General Assembly's judiciary committee is about to hold its first long night meeting of the 1989 session.

What is about to occur will have little to do with the civics lessons given by the friendly women in the red jackets.

Civics lessons do not mention pizza, beer, and jokes made funny by fatigue. They do not explain a legislative race against the clock and calendar that often forces lawmakers to substitute instinct for close analysis.

The judiciary committee is one of the legislature's busiest. By the end of the five-month session in June, the committee will have drafted, amended, approved, or killed about 500 bills—about 14 percent of the 3,649 bills filed with the Senate and House clerks.

Judiciary's 14 percent will touch nearly everyone. The committee considers matters of life and death, marriage and divorce, freedom and imprisonment.

This year's issues include surrogate parenting, birth certificates, and adoption. The death penalty and letting the terminally ill die. Longer prison sentences and home release. Committing the mentally ill to hospitals.

Handling these weighty matters is a panel that is predominantly white, male, and college-educated.

It has 27 men and three women; 18 are lawyers, one is a funeral director, another is a former FBI agent, and several are full-time legislators. Two members are black, 28 are white, and none are Hispanic.

The committee's deadline for acting on the 425 bills that had been referred to it since January is April 17, which has prompted the night meeting to begin moving business.

More bills are arriving in judiciary, sent by other committees and referred from the floors of the House and Senate.

"Everything seems to come to judiciary," said Lucy Bellone, the committee's clerk.

On Thursday night, the mood is relaxed in a second-floor meeting room in the Legislative Office Building. The committee members are seated around an oval rosewood table in gray leather swivel chairs. Two dozen lobbyists and legislative staff members watch.

Some members are more relaxed than others. The House met all day. Some legislators went out for dinner before the 8 p.m. meeting; others settled for beer or soda and take-out pizza from Casa Loma, a South End restaurant run by a former legislator, Paul LaRosa.

Rep. Richard D. Tulisano, D-Rocky Hill, a co-chairman, has his jacket off. The other co-chairman, Sen. Anthony V. Avallone, D-New Haven, is casually dressed—V-neck sweater over a shirt worn open at the collar. The Senate did not meet Thursday.

The first bill that draws debate—a "talker"—is not a matter of life or death. It is An Act Concerning the Sale of Certain Paintings. It has been dubbed the "schlock-art bill."

Intended to identify paintings that are mass-produced and passed off as originals, often in tourist areas, the bill would require such paintings to carry the label "Not original art."

Tulisano got the idea for the bill after visiting the artist colony at Rockport, Mass.

Rep. Anthony J. Nania, R-Canaan, a lawyer with salt-and-pepper hair and beard and a frequent sparring partner of Tulisano's, fired the first shot.

"Silly bill," Nania says.

Tulisano, a lively man with the build and sometimes the demeanor of Fiorello La Guardia, mayor of New York from 1933 to 1945, is neither offended nor apologetic.

"Schlock art gets schlock law," he says.

Rep. Joseph Grabarz, D-Bridgeport, is a freshman, but he immediately sees the possibilities.

"Does this affect those velvet Elvis paintings?" Grabarz asks, suppressing a smile. Everyone laughs.

"Not if they're originals," Tulisano replies.

Nania reads and rereads the bill.

"Did anybody put their name on this?" Nania asks.

"I did," Tulisano says.

"Shouldn't we send this to environment?" Grabarz asks. Sending a bill to another committee—especially one whose deadline is past, such as the environment committee—is one way to kill a bill. Everyone laughs again.

Tulisano looks up helplessly, in the fashion of comedian Jack Benny.

Finally, Tulisano says, "We'll hold it—"

Some cheer. A "hold" this late often means the bill will die.

"—until Monday."

Cheers turn to groans. Tulisano smiles. A chairman's bills, schlock or not, do not die easily.

Senate Bill 630 is titled An Act Concerning Blood Specimens and Saliva Samples of Certain Sexual Offenders. Everyone stares at their copy of the bill. This is heavy-duty. The legislation would direct the state to collect blood and saliva samples from sex offenders and to maintain the samples.

Technology has outstripped the law. It is possible to identify rapists through genetic tracking. Using semen or other bodily fluids left by rapists, scientists say they could make an identification if sex offenders had their blood and saliva samples on file.

"This has been equated to a thumbprint," Tulisano begins.

Nania tries to recall a precedent for forcing prisoners to submit blood or saliva. Others say they are troubled. They wonder if there are constitutional questions. Some are ready to vote.

"No," Tulisano says, holding up his hands in a not-so-fast gesture. "Let's talk about it."

Some nights, the committee flies by the seat of its pants on major bills. Together it will reason something out, a process that seems casual to the uninitiated. This will not be one of those nights.

"Can we have somebody look at it and bring it back next week?" Nania asks.

The committee members agree and move through the rest of the 40-item agenda.

Legislation that would use the interest on lawyers' trust accounts for legal aid is debated at length, even though nearly everyone agrees the idea is a good way to raise money to ensure legal representation for the poor.

Lawyers do not collect interest on trust accounts where clients' money is commingled. The interest is kept by the banks. The banks have not objected, and the bill would raise close to $4 million for legal aid, says Raphael "Rafie" L. Podolsky, a lawyer and lobbyist for Connecticut Legal Services.

The bar association runs a similar volunteer program. It formally has asked for another year to make it work voluntarily, but it is not strenuously fighting the legislation.

Still, the debate is lengthy. The discussion turns into a debate on legal aid lawyers and their habit of representing tenants who drag out eviction proceedings into legal nightmares. Numerous amendments are offered, some made up on the spot, and rejected.

Avallone finally has had enough. "I think we are taking a simple bill and making it complicated," he says. The bill passes, 21-7 with two absent.

"Rafie will be wearing a tuxedo Monday," one lobbyist jokes, thinking of the windfall for legal aid.

And on it goes, until the agenda and the lawmakers are exhausted at shortly after 11 p.m.

Friday morning is mop-up time. Bellone, committee clerk, and the rest of the committee staff do the paperwork that is generated by the committee's action or inaction on 40 bills. They are obviously tired. They joke about closing the office at noon.

People stop by to find out what happened to pet bills. When she has time, Bellone tells them. Lobbyists call to seek meetings with Tulisano and Avallone. She tries to accommodate them.

A staff member struggles with a computer, trying to keep the files up to date. The machine no longer recognizes her password.

"No-good piece of..." She doesn't finish the sentence.

Bellone reaches Avallone on the telephone to schedule the next meeting. Little time is spent rehashing last night. The committee's deadline is 10 days away. More bills are arriving. There is no looking back.

Annual bibliography

BY JO A. CATES

Sports writing, travel writing, and the education beat were covered in depth in 1989. In addition, Don Murray's followers should note that he has published a new book entitled *Expecting the Unexpected: Teaching Myself—and Others—to Read and Write*. The following bibliography of selected books, periodical and magazine articles, conference papers, and reports, all published in 1989, focuses on the art and craft of writing for newspapers. Also included are selected items on the teaching of writing, writing coaching, and journalistic ethics.

BOOKS

Anson, Robert S. *War News: A Young Reporter in Indochina*. New York: Simon & Schuster, 1989.

Baker, Russell. *The Good Times*. New York: Arbor House, 1989.

Biagi, Shirley. *How to Write and Sell Magazine Articles*. 2d ed. Englewood Cliffs, NJ: Prentice Hall, 1989.

Biographical Dictionary of American Journalism. Joseph P. McKerns, ed. Westport, CT: Greenwood Press, 1989.

Bisher, Furman. *The Furman Bisher Collection*. Dallas, TX: Taylor, 1989. (Sports columns originally appearing in the *Atlanta Journal and Constitution, Sport* magazine, and *Sky* magazine.)

Brooks, Brian S., and James Pinson. *Working With Words*. New York: St. Martin's Press, 1989.

Brooks, Terri. *Words Worth*. New York: St. Martin's Press, 1989.

Caswell, Lucy Shelton. *Guide to Sources in American Journalism History.* Westport, CT: Greenwood Press, 1989. (Annotated bibliography and reference guide.)

Cose, Ellis. *The Press.* New York: William Morrow, 1989.

Covering the Education Beat: A Current Guide for Editors and Writers. Lisa Walker and John Rankin, eds. Washington, D.C.: Education Writers Association, 1989.

Donovan, Hedley. *Right Places, Right Times: Forty Years in Journalism Not Counting My Paper Route.* New York: Henry Holt & Co., 1989.

Elbow, Peter, and Pat Belanoff. *A Community of Writers: A Workshop Course in Writing.* New York: Random House, 1989.

—. *Sharing and Responding.* New York: Random House, 1989.

Evans, Nigel, Philip Tremewan, and Hilary Watson. *Getting Into Print: A Journalism Textbook.* Auckland, New Zealand: New House Publishers, 1989.

Fedler, Fred. *Reporting for the Print Media.* 4th ed. New York: Harcourt Brace Jovanovich, 1989.

Gibson, Martin L. *The Writer's Friend.* Ames, IA: Iowa State University Press, 1989.

Health Risks and the Press: Perspectives on Media Coverage of Risk Assessment and Health. Mike Moore, ed. Washington, D.C.: The Media Institute in cooperation with the American Media Association, 1989.

Izenberg, Jerry. *The Jerry Izenberg Collection.* Dallas, TX: Taylor, 1989. (Sports columns originally appearing in the Newark *Star-Ledger.*)

Killenberg, George M. *Before the Story.* New York: St. Martin's Press, 1989. (On interviewing.)

Killing the Messenger: 100 Years of Media Criticism. Tom Goldstein, ed. New York: Columbia University Press, 1989.

Local Reporting, 1947-1987: From a Country Vote Fraud to a Corrupt City Council. Heinz-Dietrich Fischer and Erika J. Fischer, eds. The Pulitzer Prize Archive, v. 3. New York: K.G. Saur, 1989.

Mallon, Thomas. *Stolen Words: Essays into the Origins and Ravages of Plagiarism.* New York: Ticknor & Fields, 1989.

Milton, Joyce. *The Yellow Kids: Foreign Correspondents in the Heyday of Yellow Journalism.* New York: Harper & Row, 1989.

Murray, Donald M. *Expecting the Unexpected: Teaching Myself—and Others—to Read and Write.* Portsmouth, NH: Boynton/Cook, 1989.

Pippert, Wesley G. *An Ethics of News: A Reporter's Search for Truth.* Washington, D.C.: Georgetown University Press, 1989.

Sloan, W. David. *American Journalism History.* Westport, CT: Greenwood Press, 1989. (Annotated bibliography.)

Spander, Art. *The Art Spander Collection.* Dallas, TX: Taylor, 1989. (Sports columns originally appearing in the *San Francisco Examiner.*)

Stepp, Carl Sessions. *Editing for Today's Newsroom: New Perspectives for a Changing Profession.* Hillsdale, NJ: Lawrence Erlbaum Associates, 1989.

Strentz, Herbert. *News Reporters and News Sources: Accomplices in Shaping and Mis-*

Shaping the News. 2d ed. Ames, IA: Iowa State University Press, 1989.

Wagner, Lilya. *Women War Correspondents in World War II.* Westport, CT: Greenwood Press, 1989.

Williams, Frederick. *Computer-Assisted Writing Instruction in Journalism and Professional Education.* New York: Praeger, 1989.

Worlds of Writing: Teaching and Writing in a Variety of Discourse Communities. Carolyn Matalene, ed. New York: Random House, 1989.

PERIODICAL AND MAGAZINE ARTICLES

Abcarian, Robin. "Blending Reporting and Reflection in a Column." *The Coaches' Corner*, March 1989, pp. 1, 5.

Aleshire, Peter. "You've Got to Get People Into Your Stories." *The Coaches' Corner*, Sept. 1989, p. 3.

Anderson, Robert. "Travel Writing: A Primer." *The Writer,* June 1989, pp. 14-16.

Ausenbaugh, James D. "Stop Language Abuse!" *The Coaches' Corner*, Dec. 1989, p. 4.

Baker, Christopher P. "How to Travel the Lucrative Road of Travel Writing." *Writer's Digest,* June 1989, pp. 22-26.

Beach, Randall. "You've Got to See the People, Be in the Streets." *The Coaches' Corner,* March 1989, pp. 1, 3, 6.

Beasley, Alex, and John Huff. "Medical, Sports Writers Analyze Cost of Winning." *The Coaches' Corner*, June 1989, p. 9.

Bhatia, Peter. "Introducing 'The Write Stuff.'" *ASNE Bulletin,* Sept. 1989, p. 32.

Blais, Madeleine. "Getting Inspired by Dickens, Crane, Morrison." *The Coaches' Corner,* March 1989, p. 6.

Blundell, Bill. "Notes on the Use of Quotes." *The Coaches' Corner*, June 1989, pp. 4, 6.

Bor, Jonathon. "Taking the Reader Into a World of Secret Language." *The Coaches' Corner,* Sept. 1989, pp. 2, 10. (On medical writing.)

Bova, Ben. "Writing About Science." *Writer's Digest*, Jan. 1989, pp. 36-39.

Budd, Benita. "The Art of Being the Art Critic." *The Coaches' Corner*, June 1989, p. 8.

Buddenbaum, Judith M. "Developing Religion News, Not Religious News." *The Coaches' Corner,* Dec. 1989, pp. 1-2.

Cates, Jo. "What Reporters and Editors Should Know About Databases." *Style*, Summer 1989, pp. 20-22.

Clark, Roy Peter. "Call 'Em Prints of Darkness." *Righting Words,* March/April 1989, pp. 5-7.

Coulson, David C., and Cecilie Gaziano. "How Journalists at Two Newspapers View Good Writing and Writing Coaches." *Journalism Quarterly,* Summer 1989, pp. 435-440.

DeView, Lucille. "Capturing the Compelling Moment." *The Coaches' Corner*, Dec. 1989, p. 8.

Dunwoody, Sharon. "What's Different About Science Writing?" *The Coaches' Corner*, Sept. 1989, pp. 1, 6, 10.

Eisenberg, Steve. "Developing Focus and a Range of Sources for Science Stories." *The Coaches' Corner,* Sept. 1989, pp. 4, 12.

Flaherty, Mary Pat. "The Editor as Writing Coach." *Scripps-Howard News*, May 1989, pp. 22-23.

Fry, Don. "Coaching Editorial Writers With a New Model." *The Coaches' Corner*, March 1989, pp. 4-5.

—. "The Dreadful Joy of Newswriting." *APME News*, 15 April 1989, pp. 6-7.

—. "Kicking Out of News Stories." *The Quill*, Feb. 1989, pp. 10-11.

—. "What Do Our Interns Know About Journalism Ethics?" *Journal of Mass Media Ethics*, v. 4, no. 2, 1989, pp. 186-192.

—. "What Do You Mean, 'Make My Prose Brighter'?" *ASNE Bulletin*, Oct. 1989, pp. 12-15.

Gersh, Debra. "Furniture Salesman Wins Pulitzer Prize." *Editor & Publisher*, 8 April 1989, pp. 9-12, 34, 36, 38.

Hart, Jack. "Writing the Lead: Taking That First Long Step." *The Coaches' Corner,* Sept. 1989, pp. 8-9. (Originally published in *Second Takes,* a monthly in-house newsletter of *The Oregonian.*)

Howell, Deborah. "...Because We Treasure Writing." *English Journal*, Dec. 1989, pp. 21-26.

Jacobi, Peter P. "Writing the Personality Profile." *Folio*, April 1989, pp. 118-124.

Laakaniemi, Ray. "The Sauna Hotline: The Coach as Reporter." *The Coaches' Corner*, Dec. 1989, pp. 6-7, 8.

Laib, Nevin K. "Good Writing Cannot Be Taught Effectively as an Empty Collection of Rules." *Chronicle of Higher Education*, 5 July 1989, p. A36.

Lesher, Tina. "The Writing Coach Under a Microscope." *The Coaches' Corner,* Dec. 1989, pp. 10-11.

Logan, Robert. "Good Science Writing Starts With Skeptical Reporting." *The Coaches' Corner*, Sept. 1989, pp. 1, 10.

Malcolm, Janet. "The Journalist and the Murderer." Part 1, "The Journalist," *New Yorker*, 13 March 1989, pp. 38-73. Part 2, "The Murderer," *New Yorker*, 20 March 1989, pp. 49-82. (Malcolm's new book, *The Journalist and the Murderer*, is based on this two-part series. It was published by Knopf in 1990.)

McQuaid, E. Patrick. "A Story at Risk: The Rising Tide of Mediocre Education Coverage." *Phi Delta Kappan,* Jan. 1989, pp. K1-K8.

Mencher, Mel. "It's High Time to Emphasize Reporting." *APME News*, 15 Dec. 1989, p. 22.

Morgan, James. "Writer Meets Editor." *Writer's Digest,* May 1989, pp. 25-30.

Olson, Lyle D. "Technical Writing Methods Show Ways to Consider Audience." *Journalism Educator,* Summer 1989, pp. 3-6.

Perrin, Timothy. "Unleashing Your Creativity: Becoming a Better, More Productive Writer." *Writer's Digest*, July 1989, pp. 20-25.

Pitts, Beverly. "Model Provides Description of News Writing Process." *Journalism Educator*, Spring 1989, pp. 12-19, 59.

Reynolds, Bruce. "Editors, Reporters Need to 'Talk It Over.'" *The Coaches' Corner*, Dec. 1989, pp. 1-6.

— "Having Trouble Writing? Try These Warm-Ups." *The Coaches' Corner*, March 1989, p. 8.

Rich, Carole. "FORK: A Handy Tool to Organize Your Stories." *The Coaches' Corner,* March 1989, p. 7. (Focus, Order, Repetition of Key Words, Kiss-off.)

Spikol, Art. "Don't Shoot the Columnist. He's Only Doing His Job." *Writer's Digest*, Dec. 1989, pp. 14-16.

—. "The Road You Can Take." *Writer's Digest*, Jan. 1989, pp. 14-16.

Stocking, S. Holly, and Paget H. Gross. "Understanding Errors, Biases That Can Affect Journalists." *Journalism Educator*, Spring 1989, pp. 4-11.

Weeks, Linton. "8 Ingredients of Powerful Nonfiction." *Writer's Digest*, Sept. 1989, pp. 26-29.

Wilhoit, G. Cleveland, and Dan G. Drew. "Portrait of an Editorial Writer, 1971-88." *The Masthead*, Spring 1989, pp. 4-11.

REPORTS AND CONFERENCE PAPERS

Lipschultz, Jeremy Harris. "A Coorientational Analysis of Trial Lawyer and News Reporter Relationships." Paper presented at the annual meeting of the Association for Education in Journalism and Mass Communication, Washington, D.C., Aug. 1989, ERIC, ED 309417. 76pp.

Mackey, James. "How to Discuss Educational Research on the Opinion Page of a Newspaper." Paper presented at the colloquium on the Interdependence of Educational Research, Educational Policy, and the Press, Charlottesville, VA, Aug. 1989, ERIC, ED 310408. 12pp.

Palen, John. "'Just the Facts, Ma'am': An Inquiry into the Desirability of Fact/Value Separation in Science and Technology Controversy." Paper presented at the annual meeting of the Association for Education in Journalism and Mass Communication, Washington, D.C., Aug. 1989, ERIC, ED 308557. 36pp.

Salwen, Michael B., and Bruce Garrison. "Professional Orientations of Sports Journalists: Their Role in Journalism." Paper presented at the annual meeting of the Association for Education in Journalism and Mass Communication, Washington, D.C., Aug. 1989, ERIC, ED 309421.

Savage, David. "The Press and Education Research: Why One Ignores the Other." Paper presented at the colloquium on the Interdependence of Educational Research, Educational Policy, and the Press, Charlottesville, VA, Aug. 1989, ERIC, ED 311464. 37pp.

Woodress, Frederick A. "Criminals Assess Their Treatment by the Media." Paper presented at the annual meeting of the Association for Education in Journalism and Mass Communication, Washington, D.C., Aug. 1989, ERIC, ED 310458. 17pp.